Workbook 2 • Lessons 16-30
www.basicesl.com/workbook-2

For beginner English language learners

SESMA
BilingualDictionaries.com

Basic ESL® Workbook 2
English as a Second Language Program
3rd Edition

Publisher:

Bilingual Dictionaries, Inc.
P.O. Box 1154
Murrieta, CA 92564
Website: www.bilingualdictionaries.com
Email: support@bilingualdictionaries.com

Original Content by C. Sesma, M.A.
English and Spanish Teacher

Designed and Edited by Bilingual Dictionaries, Inc.
Alex Sesma • Editor, Content, Design
Kevin Cole • Content, ESL Teacher
Jose Quezada • Design, Illustrations

ISBN13: 978-1-946986-98-6
ISBN10: 1-946986-98-4

For **information, downloads** and **videos** please visit the Basic ESL® website:
Website: www.basicesl.com
Email: support@basicesl.com

Printed in the USA

Basic ESL Workbook

Basic ESL introduces grammar and writing to beginner English language learners. Students improve their English skills through simple examples and exercises. Each lesson includes a topic for vocabulary and introduces a basic grammar concept. The workbook exercises are built around each lesson's vocabulary and grammar examples. This provides students an opportunity to practice sentence structure and vocabulary together in a meaningful way. The workbooks are an excellent resource for students to practice writing skills and improve their English.

The 45 lessons are designed to give beginner students a lesson-by-lesson path for improving their English. Each lesson builds on the previous lesson's vocabulary and grammar. After completing all 3 workbooks, students will have covered multiple parts of speech, different tenses, modals and much more.

3 Workbooks • 45 lessons

There are three workbooks with 15 lessons each. The complete workbook series includes 45 lessons.

- Workbook 1: Lessons 1-15
- Workbook 2: Lessons 16-30
- Workbook 3: Lessons 31-45

Instructions

We encourage students to complete the lessons in order and with the help of a teacher, tutor or friend.

1. Review lesson vocabulary and grammar
2. Watch the lesson videos
3. Complete the exercises in the workbook
4. Download extra exercises

Videos and Downloads | basicesl.com | YouTube

Each workbook lesson features English pronunciation videos to practice the lesson vocabulary and grammar. The vocabulary and grammar examples in the videos are identical to the workbooks. The examples are presented in order, through an easy-to-understand listen-and-repeat format. The videos are an excellent resource for students to practice listening, reading, and speaking skills.

Extra downloads including extra exercise worksheets and lesson quizzes are also available. Visit our website to find all the extra resources that go along with each lesson. Become a basicesl.com member to download worksheets and get discount pricing on workbooks and bilingual dictionaries.

- Vocabulary Videos
- Grammar Videos
- Exercise Videos
- Vocabulary Exercises
- Grammar Exercises
- Lesson Quizzes
- Workbooks
- Dictionaries

Contact Us

Please contact us with any questions, comments or suggestions. Call or email us:

(951)-296-2445 • support@basicesl.com
Monday - Friday • 7 a.m. to 3 p.m.

Dear Teachers & Students

We thank you for your continued support. You are appreciated. Please send us any feedback or suggestions. We are listening.

We wish you the best, and a bright future!

Table of Contents

Table of Contents

Irregular Verbs

Base Form	Simple Past	Past Participle
arise	arose	arisen
awake	awoke	awoken
be	was/were	been
bear	bore	born(e)
beat	beat	beaten
become	became	become
begin	began	begun
bend	bent	bent
bet	bet	bet
bind	bound	bound
bite	bit	bitten
bleed	bled	bled
blow	blew	blown
break	broke	broken
breed	bred	bred
bring	brought	brought
broadcast	broadcast	broadcast
build	built	built
burn	burnt/burned	burnt/burned
burst	burst	burst
buy	bought	bought
can	could	… (been able)
catch	caught	caught
choose	chose	chosen
cling	clung	clung
come	came	come
cost	cost	cost
creep	crept	crept
cut	cut	cut
deal	dealt	dealt
dig	dug	dug
do	did	done
draw	drew	drawn
dream	dreamt/dreamed	dreamt/dreamed
drink	drank	drunk

Base Form	Simple Past	Past Participle
drive	drove	driven
eat	ate	eaten
fall	fell	fallen
feed	fed	fed
feel	felt	felt
fight	fought	fought
find	found	found
fit	fit	fit
fly	flew	flown
forbid	forbade	forbidden
forget	forgot	forgotten
forgive	forgave	forgiven
freeze	froze	frozen
get	got	got
give	gave	given
go	went	gone
grind	ground	ground
grow	grew	grown
hang	hung	hung
have	had	had
hear	heard	heard
hide	hid	hidden
hit	hit	hit
hold	held	held
hurt	hurt	hurt
keep	kept	kept
kneel	knelt	knelt
know	knew	known
lay	laid	laid
lead	led	led
lean	leant/leaned	leant/leaned
learn	learnt/learned	learnt/learned
leave	left	left
lent	lent	lent
lie *(in bed)*	lay	lain

Irregular Verbs

Base Form	Simple Past	Past Participle
lie *(not truth)*	lied	lied
light	lit/lighted	lit/lighted
lose	lost	lost
make	made	made
may	might	…
mean	meant	meant
meet	met	met
mow	mowed	mown/mowed
must	had to	…
overtake	overtook	overtaken
pay	paid	paid
put	put	put
read	read	read
ride	rode	ridden
ring	rang	rung
rise	rose	risen
run	ran	run
saw	sawed	sawn/sawed
say	said	said
see	saw	seen
sell	sold	sold
send	sent	sent
set	set	set
sew	sewed	sewn/sewed
shake	shook	shaken
shall	should	…
shed	shed	shed
shine	shone	shone
shoot	shot	shot
show	showed	shown
shrink	shrank	shrunk
shut	shut	shut
sing	sang	sung
sink	sank	sunk
sit	sat	sat

Base Form	Simple Past	Past Participle
sleep	slept	slept
slide	slid	slid
smell	smelt	smelt
sow	sowed	sown/sowed
speak	spoke	spoken
spell	spelt/spelled	spelt/spelled
spend	spent	spent
spill	spilt/spilled	spilt/spilled
spit	spat	spat
spread	spread	spread
stand	stood	stood
steal	stole	stolen
stick	stuck	stuck
sting	stung	stung
stink	stank	stunk
strike	struck	struck
swear	swore	sworn
sweep	swept	swept
swell	swelled	swollen/swelled
swim	swam	swum
swing	swung	swung
take	took	taken
teach	taught	taught
tear	tore	torn
tell	told	told
think	thought	thought
throw	threw	thrown
understand	understood	understood
wake	woke	woken
wear	wore	worn
weep	wept	wept
will	would	…
win	won	won
wind	wound	wound
write	wrote	written

basicesl.com

Lessons = Workbooks + Videos

We provide English pronunciation videos for all of our vocabulary and grammar examples. Our videos give students a chance to listen and repeat the sentence structures found in each lesson.

Videos found on **basicesl.com** are student friendly, with no ads or commercials.

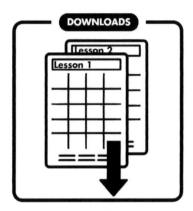

Members = Downloads + Discounts

Extra downloads are available online. Join **basicesl.com** to download additional exercises.

- Vocabulary worksheets
- Grammar worksheets
- Quiz worksheets

Member 1 = Downloads

Member 2 = Downloads + Workbooks

Member 3 = Downloads + Workbooks + Discount

Workbooks and Dictionaries

Find our workbooks and bilingual dictionaries at **basicesl.com.** Discount members receive an online shopping discount. Bilingual dictionaries are a great tool for English language learners.

Basic ESL Workbooks along with bilingual dictionaries are great tools for teachers that have ESL students with different native languages.

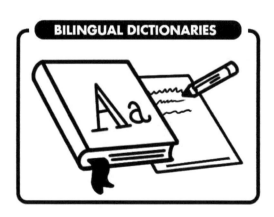

Workbook 2
Food
Lesson 16: Fruits & Vegetables

Indefinite adjectives *some* and *any*
Using *there is* and *there are*

 basicesl.com/workbook-2/lesson-16

☐	Watch vocabulary video. Listen and repeat.
☐	Complete vocabulary exercises. (**Download**)
☐	Watch grammar video. Listen and repeat.
☐	Complete grammar exercises. (**Workbook**)
☐	Complete extra grammar exercises. (**Download**)
☐	Take a quiz. (**Download**)

Vocabulary

1. apple	**2.** banana	**3.** grape	**4.** orange
5. pineapple	**6.** strawberry	**7.** watermelon	**8.** coconut
9. lemon	**10.** cherry	**11.** lettuce	**12.** broccoli
13. onion	**14.** tomato	**15.** pepper	**16.** cucumber
17. corn	**18.** carrot	**19.** mushroom	**20.** potato

21. fruit (*noun*)   **22.** vegetable (*noun*)   **23.** juicy (*adj*)

24. sweet (*adj*)   **25.** sour (*adj*)   **26.** to offer (*verb*)

27. to prepare (*verb*)   **28.** to give (*verb**)   **29.** to eat (*verb**)

* Irregular verb list page 6

Indefinite adjectives *some* and *any*

Statement	Negative statement
I buy **some** yellow bananas.	I don't buy **any** green bananas.
She has **some** carrots.	She doesn't have **any** corn.
We need **some** fruit.	We don't need **any** vegetables.
They get **some** apples.	They don't get **any** oranges.

Question	Answer
Do you prepare **any** potatoes?	Yes, I prepare **some** potatoes. No, I don't prepare **any** potatoes.
Does he like **any** vegetables?	Yes, he likes **some** vegetables. No, he doesn't like **any** vegetables.
Do they eat **any** onion?	Yes, they eat **some** onion. No, they don't eat **any** onion.

Questions with *some*	Answer
Do you want **some** watermelon?	Yes, I want **some** watermelon. No, I don't want **any** watermelon.
Are you looking for **some** grapes?	Yes, I'm looking for **some** grapes. No, I'm not looking for **any** grapes.

The indefinite adjectives *some* and *any* are used when the exact amount or number of something is unknown.

Use *some* in statements. Use *any* in negative statements and questions.

Sometimes we use *some* instead of *any* in questions. For example, we often use *some* in offers when the expected answer is *yes*.

It is common to use *some* in questions when the expected answer is *yes*. An offer is a common question where the expected answer is *yes*..

Using *there is* and *there are*

Statement	Negative statement
There is lettuce.	**There is** no lettuce.
There is some broccoli.	**There is** not any broccoli.
There are sweet onions.	**There are** no sweet onions.
There are some red cherries.	**There are** not any red cherries.

Question	Answer
Is there corn for Tom?	Yes, **there is** corn for Tom. No, **there isn't** corn for Tom.
Are there any juicy oranges?	Yes, **there are** some juicy oranges. No, **there aren't** any juicy oranges.
Is there any lemon in that?	Yes, **there is** some lemon in this. No, **there is** no lemon in this.
Are there peppers in the bowl?	Yes, **there are** some peppers. No, **there aren't** any peppers.

We use the adverb *there* and the verb *to be* when something exists or is available.

Singular	Plural
There *is*	**There** *are*

There are two ways to express negative statements with *there* and *to be*.

There *is* no	**There** *are* no
There *isn't* any	**There** *aren't* any

To ask if something exists or is available, the verb *to be* goes before the word *there*.

Is **there**	*Are* **there**

Exercises

A: Complete the sentence with **some** or **any**.

1. You have ___some___ potatoes.

   Do you have _____ tomatoes?

   No, I don't have _____ .

2. You don't need _____ mushrooms.

   Do you need _____ cucumbers?

   Yes, I need _____ cucumbers.

3. Does the store have _____ broccoli?

   No, it doesn't have _____ broccoli.

   It doesn't have _____ lettuce.

4. Do you want _____ corn? **(offer)**

   Yes, I want _____ corn.

   I don't want _____ fruit.

5. Do you have _____ vegetables?

   No, I don't have _____ vegetables.

   Do you want _____ vegetables? **(offer)**

6. Do we need _____ onions?

   No, we don't need _____ .

   Do you want _____ onions? **(offer)**

B: Change the statement to a **question**. Use the verb **to be**.

1. There are apples.   ___Are there apples?___

2. There is lettuce.   _____

3. There are potatoes in the cupboard. _____

4. There are green apples.   _____

5. There are some grapes for Jill. _____

6. There is lemon in the water. _____

7. There is a banana in the kitchen. _____

8. There are strawberries in this drink. _____

9. There is some onion in the food. _____

10. There is some fruit on the table. _____

C: Write two **negative** statements. Do not use contractions. Follow the example.

1. There are vegetables.

   *There **are no** vegetables.*

   *There **are not any** vegetables.*

2. There are apples and oranges.

3. There is juicy watermelon.

4. There is lemon in the cup.

5. There are sweet cherries in the bowl.

D: Write **yes** and **no** answers with **some** or **any**. Use <u>subject pronouns</u> and **contractions**.

1. Do I like any of the peppers?

   *Yes, <u>you</u> like **some** of the peppers.*

   *No, <u>you</u> **don't** like **any** of the peppers.*

2. Does the restaurant prepare any potatoes?

3. Does the store offer coconuts today?

4. Do the boys get any oranges?

5. Does Mary have any sweet potatoes?

6. Do you and Tom want some of my grapes?

Exercises

1. apples / kitchen

*Are there any **apples** in the kitchen?*

*__No__, there **aren't any** apples in the kitchen.*

*Are there any **bananas**?*

*__Yes__, there **are some** bananas.*

2. potatoes / plate

3. pepper / pan

4. cherries / refrigerator

5. watermelon / bowl

F: Follow the example.

1. to eat

Henry	Mary

*Do they eat any **carrots**?*

***Henry eats** some carrots.*

Mary doesn't eat any carrots.

2. to sell

Mark	Lisa

3. to get

Ann	Paul

4. to want **(offer)**

boys	girls

5. to have

Alex	Seth

Exercises

1. Mary does not have _vegetables_____ in her refrigerator.

           a. vegetables   **b.** oranges   **c.** grapes

2. Which fruit does Mary have in her refrigerator?

           a. pineapple   **b.** grapes   **c.** oranges

3. Mary wants some _____ .

           a. carrots   **b.** broccoli   **c.** a & b

4. Mary doesn't want any _____ .

           a. mushrooms   **b.** onions   **c.** a & b

5. Mary goes to her favorite store _____ a week.

           a. once   **b.** two times   **c.** three times

6. The vegetables at her favorite store are _____ .

           a. not cheap.   **b.** not expensive

7. The store doesn't have any _____ peppers.

           a. green   **b.** red   **c.** yellow

8. Mary buys carrots, broccoli and _____ .

           a. grapes   **b.** pineapple   **c.** watermelon

Workbook 2
Food
Lesson 17: Food & Drink
Count and non-count nouns
Using quantifiers

 basicesl.com/workbook-2/lesson-17

- ☐ Watch vocabulary video. Listen and repeat.
- ☐ Complete vocabulary exercises. (**Download**)
- ☐ Watch grammar video. Listen and repeat.
- ☐ Complete grammar exercises. (**Workbook**)
- ☐ Complete extra grammar exercises. (**Download**)
- ☐ Take a quiz. (**Download**)

Vocabulary

1. meat	**2.** egg	**3.** fish	**4.** cheese
5. water	**6.** wine	**7.** coffee	**8.** juice
9. milk	**10.** tea	**11.** pasta	**12.** sauce
13. beans	**14.** rice	**15.** bread	**16.** butter
17. salt	**18. pepper**	**19.** sugar	**20.** honey

21. ice (*noun*)

22. type (*noun*)

23. piece (*noun*)

24. slice (*noun*)

25. hungry (*adj*)

26. thirsty (*adj*)

27. to drink (*verb**)

28. to spill (*verb*)

29. to pour (*verb*)

* Irregular verb list page 6

Count and non-count nouns

Count nouns are nouns that can be counted with a number. They have singular and plural forms.

Non-count nouns usually do not have a plural form. They can not be counted. Non-count nouns use quantifiers or other words to describe the amount.

Count nouns

apple	Do you want **an apple**?	Yes, I want **four apples**.
egg	Does he get **any eggs**?	Yes, he gets **3 eggs**.
tomato	Does she grab **a tomato**?	Yes, she grabs **two tomatoes**.
carrot	Do they find **any carrots**?	Yes, they find **10 carrots**.

Non-count noun

coffee	Do you want **some coffee**?	Yes, I want **a cup** of **coffee**.
honey	Does he use **any honey**?	Yes, he uses **a spoon** of **honey**.
wine	Does she want **some wine**?	Yes, she wants **some wine**.
cheese	Does it have **any cheese**?	Yes, it has **two slices** of **cheese**.
pasta	Do they prepare **any pasta**?	Yes, they prepare **some pasta**.
cake	Does he want **some cake**?	Yes, he wants **two pieces** of **cake**.
water	Do they need **any tea**?	Yes, they need **a pot** of **tea**.
milk	Do you sell **any fish**?	Yes, we sell **3 types** of **fish**.

Using quantifiers

The quantifiers *few* and *many* are used with count nouns.

Quantifiers are used when the exact amount or number of a noun is unknown. Below are some common quantifiers.

Question	Answer
How **many** bananas are there?	There aren't **many** bananas.
How **many** grapes does she eat?	She eats **a few** grapes.
How **many** lemons do they buy?	They don't buy **many** lemons.
Do you have **a few** onions?	Yes, I have **a few** onions.

Count

a few: a small number

many: a large number (common in negative statements and questions)

The quantifiers *a little* and *much* are used with non-count nouns.

Question	Answer
How **much** rice is there?	There isn't **much** rice.
How **much** salt do we use?	We use **a little** salt.
How **much** milk do you pour?	I don't pour **much** milk.
Do you want **a little** butter?	Yes, I want **a little** butter.

Non-count

a little: a small amount

much: a large amount (common in negative statements and questions)

The quantifiers *a lot, enough, plenty, some* and *any* are used for any noun.

Question	Answer
Does Dave have **enough** pasta?	Yes, he has **plenty** of pasta.
Does he want **any** vegetables?	Yes, he wants **a lot** of carrots.
Are you buying **some** fruit?	Yes, I'm buying **a lot** of fruit.
Does the store have **any** coconuts?	Yes, it has **plenty** of coconuts.
Do you drink **a lot** of water?	No, I don't drink **enough** water.
What do you drink **a lot** of?	I drink **plenty** of juice and coffee.

Both count and non-count

a lot: a large amount or number

enough: as much or as many as needed

plenty: more than enough

some or **any:** an unknown number or amount, more than one

Exercises

A: Write **count** or **non-count** for each noun.

1. salt _non-count_

2. honey _____

3. apple _____

4. pineapple _____

5. pepper _____

6. egg _____

7. pasta _____

8. cherry _____

9. food _____

10. cake _____

11. bean _____

12. juice _____

13. corn _____

14. rice _____

15. banana _____

16. lettuce _____

17. cucumber _____

18. potato _____

19. orange _____

20. meat _____

B: Complete the sentence with the **much** or **many**.

1. She doesn't pour _much_ tea.

2. I don't have _____ pineapples.

3. How _____ honey is there?

4. There isn't _____ honey on the shelf.

5. How _____ types of sauces are there?

6. How _____ children are eating?

7. How _____ pasta do you want?

8. There are _____ children eating.

9. There aren't _____ green apples.

10. There isn't _____ juice at home.

C: Complete the sentence with the **a little** or **a few**.

1. She is pouring _a little_ coffee.

2. I have _____ bananas.

3. I eat _____ eggs before school.

4. There is _____ cheese on the pasta.

5. I like _____ honey on my toast.

6. Grandfather loves _____ wine at night.

7. She is cooking _____ potatoes.

8. Dan wants _____ sauce on his pasta.

9. There are _____ types of sauces.

10. She is drinking _____ water.

Exercises

D: Write the question for the given answer using **much** or **many**.

1. ___How much_ cheese is there?___   There is **a lot of cheese.**

2. _____   I eat **plenty of cheese.**

3. _____   I am eating **a little cheese.**

4. _____   There are **a few potatoes.**

5. _____   I wash **a lot potatoes.**

6. _____   I am washing **twenty potatoes.**

7. _____   He has **enough pasta.**

8. _____   There is **a little milk.**

9. _____   I want **three eggs.**

10. _____   I want **a lot of bread.**

E: Complete each sentence with **many**, **much,** or the given **quantifier**.

1. a lot of

How ___much___ juice does Tony buy?

He buys ___a lot of___ juice.

He doesn't buy _____ tea.

2. a little

How _____ wine does Tom drink?

He doesn't drink _____ wine.

He drinks _____ wine on his birthday.

3. plenty

There is _____ of cake.

How _____ cake does Tammy want?

She doesn't want _____ cake.

4. a few

Do you want _____ grapes?

Yes, how _____ do you have?

I have _____ grapes in this small cup.

Exercises

F: Follow the example.

1. plenty / Tom
to want / a little

Is there any rice?

There is <u>plenty</u> of rice.

How much *rice does Tom want?*

He wants <u>a little</u> rice.

2. a lot of / you
to eat / a few

3. a little / the teachers
to drink / a lot of

4. a lot of / the girls
to get / a few

5. plenty / grandmother
to prepare / enough

G: Read the story and answer the questions. Use complete sentences. Follow the example.

My name is Emily. My husband Alan and I have three sons and one daughter. We eat in the kitchen every morning. We eat in the dining room every night. There is always plenty of food for our family.

My husband likes meat. Alan eats a lot of fish. He likes some vegetables. Carrots are his favorite. He doesn't eat much fruit. Alan drinks a lot of coffee. He drinks two cups of coffee in the morning and two cups at night. He takes his coffee with a spoon of sugar and a little milk.

My children love fruits and vegetables. I like to buy a lot of apples, oranges and grapes for my children. Today I am going to buy some pineapples. I need to buy a few onions and some tomatoes for tonight. We are having pasta and tomato sauce.

1. How many children do <u>Emily and Alan</u> have?

<u>They</u> have four children.

2. Where does the family eat at night?

_____

3. What is Alan's favorite vegetable?

_____

4. How many cups of coffee does Alan drink in a day?

_____

5. How does Alan take his coffee?

_____

6. What fruit is Emily buying today?

_____

7. What fruits and vegetables does Emily need for tonight?

_____

_____

Exercises

G: Listen to the story and choose the correct answer.
Visit **www.basicesl.com/workbook-2/lesson-17** to listen to the story.

1. Jane 's dinner guests are her ___clothes___ .

           a. sisters   **b.** brothers   **c.** parents

2. Jane is preparing _____ and potatoes.

           a. carrots   **b.** meat   **c.** cheese

3. Jane's mother is eating bread with _____ cheese.

           a. a lot of   **b.** a few   **c.** a little

4. Jane's father is in the _____.

           a. living room   **b.** kitchen   **c.** garage

5. Jane's father isn't drinking _____ .

           a. coffee   **b.** tea   **c.** wine

6. Jane has _____of good food for dinner.

           a. plenty   **b.** not much   **c.** a little

7. Jane put a big bowl of _____ on the table.

           a. bread   **b.** watermelon   **c.** sugar

8. Jane doesn't have _____ coffee.

           a. many   **b.** much   **c.** any

Workbook 2
Food
Lesson 18: Cooking

Simple present spelling rules

Using the question word *why*

Present tense review

 basicesl.com/workbook-2/lesson-18

☐	Watch vocabulary video. Listen and repeat.
☐	Complete vocabulary exercises. (**Download**)
☐	Watch grammar video. Listen and repeat.
☐	Complete grammar exercises. (**Workbook**)
☐	Complete extra grammar exercises. (**Download**)
☐	Take a quiz. (**Download**)

Vocabulary

1. fire	2. grill	3. toaster	4. blender
5. to peel *an orange*	6. to sprinkle *salt*	7. to cut* *cheese*	8. to slice a *banana*
9. to chop *an onion*	10. to boil *water*	11. to melt *butter*	12. to fry *an egg*
13. to stir *coffee*	14. to bake *bread*	15. to toast *bread*	16. to mix *fruit*
17. to blend *juice*	18. to grind *pepper*	19. to heat *food*	20. to grill *meat*

21. ready (*adj*)   **22.** delicious (*adj*)   **23.** ripe (*adj*)

24. spicy (*adj*)   **25.** to cook (*verb*)   **26.** to try (*verb*)

27. to make (*verb**)   **28.** to burn (*verb*)   **29.** to freeze (*verb**)

* Irregular verb list page 6

Simple present spelling rules

For most verbs, add *-s*

cook ➔ cook**s**	bake ➔ bake**s**
blend ➔ blend**s**	boil ➔ boil**s**
Kate **cooks** in her kitchen.	The oven **bakes** the bread.
Tina **blends** fruit in the blender.	John **boils** water on the stove.

For verbs ending in *-h, -s, -x, -z, -ch, -sh* or *-o*, add *-es*

go ➔ go**es**	wash ➔ wash**es**
mix ➔ mix**es**	cross ➔ cross**es**
The bread **goes** in the toaster.	Ann **washes** the pots and pans.
Ruby **mixes** the fruit.	Toby **crosses** the street.

For verbs ending in a *consonant + -y*, change the *-y* to *-ies*.

try ➔ tr**ies**	fry ➔ fr**ies**
cry ➔ cr**ies**	study ➔ stud**ies**
Ann **tries** a new wine every week.	Alan **fries** eggs in the pan.
The baby **cries** a lot.	Greg **studies** at school.

There are common spelling rules for regular verbs used with 3rd person singular subjects. For most regular verbs, add *-s* to the verb. Other spelling rules depend on the ending of the verb.

most verbs ➔ *-s*
ends in *-h, -s, -x, -z, -ch, -sh, -o* ➔ *-es*
ends in consonant + *-y* ➔ *-ies*

Using the question word *why*

Why are the bananas green?
The bananas are green **because they are not ripe.**

Why does the butter melt?
The butter melts **because the pan is over the fire.**

Why is Melissa baking a cake?
Melissa is baking a cake **because today is Ann's birthday.**

The question word *why* is used to ask for a specific reason.

To answer a *why* question use the word *because* followed by the reason.

Present tense review

Simple present
When do you **use** the blender?	I **use** the blender every day.
Who **chops** the onions?	Danny **chops** the onions.
Where does she **cook** the meat?	She **cooks** the meat on the grill.

Present continuous
What **are** you **blending** now?	I **am blending** fruit and milk.
What **is** Jenny **baking** now?	She **is baking** delicious bread.
What **are** they **grilling** for dinner?	They **are grilling** a lot of fish.

Imperatives
How do I heat the pasta?	**Heat** the pasta in the microwave.
Where do I get the water?	**Get** the water from the sink.
Which watermelon do I slice?	**Slice** the ripe one on the counter.

The simple present is used to express a truth or an action that happens regularly.

The present continuous is used to express actions happening now or at the given moment.

An imperative sentence is a command or suggestion. The subject of an imperative sentence is always *you*.

Exercises

A: Write the present tense **3rd person singular** verb form.

1. pour _pours_

2. slice _____

3. mix _____

4. blend _____

5. wash _____

6. fry _____

7. teach _____

8. grind _____

9. heat _____

10. grill _____

11. freeze _____

12. finish _____

13. try _____

14. choose _____

15. study _____

16. have _____

17. ask _____

18. use _____

19. go _____

20. do _____

B: Fill in the blanks. Use the words in the **word bank**. Use each word one time.

1. Tom ____heats____ his food in the microwave.

2. Sarah _____ her bread in the oven.

3. It _____ the strawberries and the milk.

4. She _____ her tea with a spoon.

5. Jim _____ meat outside on Sunday.

6. Katy _____ the potatoes with a knife.

7. My mother _____ the eggs in water.

8. Jose _____ his beans and rice in a bowl.

9. Your father _____ the egg in a pan.

10. Tim _____ a little pepper on his fish.

C: Read the story and answer the questions. Use complete sentences.

Tom is hungry. He wants a few eggs and a piece of toast. Tom puts two eggs and a little milk into a bowl. He mixes the eggs with a large spoon. Tom heats a pan with a little butter on the stove. He melts the butter for his eggs. After the butter melts, Tom pours the eggs into the pan. He fries the eggs for two minutes. Tom sprinkles his eggs with salt because eggs are tasty with salt. He put some cheese on top of the eggs. Tom puts a slice of bread in the toaster. The bread toasts for a few minutes. He peels an orange. Tom eats his food at the dining room table.

1. Why does Tom want eggs?

Tom wants eggs because he is hungry.

2. What does Tom put into a bowl?

3. How does Tom mix the eggs?

4. When does Tom pour the eggs into the pan?

5. How long does Tom fry the eggs?

6. Why does Tom sprinkle his eggs with salt?

7. What fruit does Tom peel?

8. Where does Tom eat his food?

Exercises

D: Follow the example.

1. Tom / <u>he is hungry</u>

What *is Tom grilling?*

He is grilling fish.

Why *is Tom grilling fish?*

He is grilling fish <u>because he is hungry</u>.

2. you / there is no meat

3. Sally / she likes toast

4. Aunt Mary / it's Ann's birthday

5. Carl / the pasta is ready

Exercises

E: Write three present tense statements using the given words. Follow the example.

1. Tom / to wash / pots

Tom **washes** *the pots.*

He **is washing** *the pots.*

Wash *the pots.*

2. Ann / to mix / fruit

3. I / to pour / milk

4. Ron / to study / library

5. oven / to bake / bread

6. Karen / to fry / eggs

7. you and Sonny / to boil / water

8. Jill and I / to chop / onions

9. chefs / to grill / meat

10. grandmother / to freeze / fish

Exercises

F: Change *sisters* to *sister* and rewrite the story.

My sisters cook my favorite food on Saturdays. They make spicy fish with white rice.

They cut large pieces of fish. They sprinkle salt and pepper on the fish. After they prepare the fish, my sisters put the rice in boiling water. They cook rice in their big pot. They melt the butter on a hot pan. My sisters fry the fish with peppers and onions.

Before we eat, my sisters mix the rice, fish, peppers and onions in a bowl.

_____

_____

_____

_____

_____

_____

_____

_____

_____

_____

G: Listen to the story and choose the correct answer.
Visit **www.basicesl.com/workbook-2/lesson-18** to listen to the story.

1. Jane's family __*bakes*__ a cake every week.   **a.** bakes   **b.** cooks   **c.** fries

2. Jane's mother's favorite cake is _____ cake.   **a.** apple   **b.** carrot   **c.** fruit

3. Jane's mother uses _____ apples for her cakes.   **a.** sweet   **b.** red   **c.** tasty

4. Jane's sister loves birthday cake with _____.   **a.** coconut   **b.** orange   **c.** sugar

5. Jane's sister takes birthday cake to _____.   **a.** church   **b.** hospital   **c.** school

6. Jane's favorite cake to make is _____ cake.   **a.** carrot   **b.** coconut   **c.** fruit

7. Jane uses _____ eggs in her cake.   **a.** three   **b.** four   **c.** five

8. Right now Jane is _____ carrots for her cake.   **a.** blending   **b.** chopping   **c.** cooking

Workbook 2
Meals
Lesson 19: Breakfast, Lunch & Dinner

Past tense statements with the verb *to be*

Past tense questions with the verb *to be*

 basicesl.com/workbook-2/lesson-19

☐   Watch vocabulary video. Listen and repeat.

☐   Complete vocabulary exercises. (**Download**)

☐   Watch grammar video. Listen and repeat.

☐   Complete grammar exercises. (**Workbook**)

☐   Complete extra grammar exercises. (**Download**)

☐   Take a quiz. (**Download**)

Vocabulary

1. cereal	**2.** bacon	**3.** ham	**4.** toast
5. pancakes	**6.** omelet	**7.** hamburger	**8.** fries
9. pizza	**10.** sandwich	**11.** soup	**12.** salad
13. steak	**14.** chicken	**15.** tuna	**16.** shrimp
17. chocolate	**18.** ice cream	**19.** pie	**20.** dessert

21. breakfast (*noun*)　　　**22.** lunch (*noun*)　　　**23.** dinner (*noun*)

24. yesterday (*noun, adv*)　**25.** fried (*adj*)　　　**26.** grilled (*adj*)

27. baked (*adj*)　　　　　　**28.** greasy (*adj*)　　　**29.** salty (*adj*)

* Irregular verb list page 6

Grammar

Past tense statements with the verb *to be*

Present	Past
I *am* here for breakfast.	I **was** here for breakfast.
You *are* in the kitchen.	You **were** in the kitchen.
He *is* thirsty before lunch.	He **was** thirsty before lunch.
She *is* hungry today.	She **was** hungry today.
It *is* spicy shrimp.	It **was** spicy shrimp.
We *are* excited for pizza.	We **were** excited for pizza.
They *are* baked potatoes.	They **were** baked potatoes.

Statement	Negative statement
I **was** here for breakfast.	I **was** *not* here for lunch.
You **were** in the kitchen.	You **were** *not* at the table.
He **was** thirsty before lunch.	He **wasn't** thirsty after lunch.
She **was** hungry today.	She **was** *not* hungry yesterday.
It **was** spicy shrimp.	It **wasn't** sweet shrimp.
We **were** excited for pizza.	We **were** *not* excited for salad.
They **were** baked potatoes.	They **weren't** fried potatoes.

The simple past tense is used to talk about things that happened before now. The past tense forms of the verb *to be* are *was* and *were*.

Singular	Plural
I **was**	We **were**
You **were**	You **were**
He **was**	They **were**
She **was**	
It **was**	

The word *not* after the verb *to be* is used to make negative statements. Contractions are made with the verb *to be* and the word *not*.

was *not* → **wasn't**

were *not* → **weren't**

Past tense questions with the verb *to be*

Statement	Question
I **was** correct.	**Was** I correct?
You **were** wrong.	**Were** you wrong?
He **was** handsome.	**Was** he handsome?
She **was** pretty.	**Was** she pretty?
It **was** salty and greasy.	**Was** it salty and greasy?
We **were** here yesterday.	**Were** we here yesterday?
They **were** there this morning.	**Were** they there this morning?

Question	Answer
Were you at home for lunch?	No, I **wasn't** at home for lunch.
Who **was** at home for lunch?	Mother **was** at home for lunch.
Was there any salad for dinner?	No, there **wasn't** any salad.
What **was** there for dinner?	There **was** soup for dinner.
Was there enough apple pie?	Yes, there **was** plenty of pie.
When **was** the pie baked?	It **was** baked yesterday.
Were the fries delicious?	No, the fries **weren't** good.
Where **were** the fries from?	They **were** from Al's Restaurant.

Past tense questions with the verb *to be* are formed by placing the verb *to be* in front of the subject. The past tense forms of the verb *to be* are *was* and *were*.

Singular	Plural
Was I	**Were** we
Were you	**Were** you
Was he	**Were** they
Was she	
Was it	

Exercises

A: Complete the **past tense** sentence with the verb **to be**.

1. The pizza ___was___ good.

2. _____ the tomatoes bad?

3. They _____ not happy with the fries.

4. _____ the chicken baked?

5. You _____ not here for lunch.

6. Dinner _____ delicious.

7. The cereal _____ in the cupboard.

8. _____ there sugar for the guests?

9. When _____ we at his restaurant?

10. John's blender _____ expensive.

11. The children _____ thirsty.

12. Who_____ the lemon juice for?

13. The pineapple pieces _____ sweet.

14. Our grill _____ a little dirty.

15. _____ the glasses clean or dirty?

16. The drink _____ extra large.

17. Those fried shrimp _____ messy.

18. What _____ there for dessert?

19. There _____ a few types of cheese.

20. _____ there any cheese at the store?

B: Change the statement to the **past tense**. Use <u>subject pronouns</u>.

1. John is at the restaurant.   ___He **was** at the restaurant.___

2. I am in the cafeteria.   _____

3. The steaks are expensive.   _____

4. Tim and I are at the store.   _____

5. The pies are inside the oven.   _____

6. You are in the back of the kitchen.   _____

7. The ice cream is in the dessert aisle.   _____

8. Customers are at the meat counter.   _____

9. The cereal is behind the coffee.   _____

10. You are at the table.   _____

Exercises

C: Write a present and past tense statement. Use the words *today* and *yesterday*. Use contractions with **not**.

1. to be-restaurant-closed

The restaurant **is** closed **today**.

_It_ **was** closed **yesterday**.

2. not-Mary-hungry-to be

3. sweet-to be-rice-not

4. beans-not-to be-John's-spicy

5. Katy-thirsty-to be-I

6. grilled-not-shrimp-to be

7. to be-lemons-juicy-not

8. delicious-to be-coffee

9. grill-to be-not-on

10. fries-not-to be-salty

Exercises

D: Change the statement to a **past** tense **question**.

1. The eggs are fried.   *Were the eggs fried?*

2. The chicken is ready.   _____

3. The grapes are ripe.   _____

4. The hamburgers are delicious.   _____

5. It is next to the salt and pepper.   _____

6. The bread is on top of the shelf.   _____

7. There is a knife on the counter.   _____

8. Our grill is behind the garage.   _____

9. This butter is expensive.   _____

10. There are pans in the sink.   _____

E: Write past tense statements with **to be.** Use contractions for negative statements. Follow the example.

1. good / bad

*The strawberries **were good.***

*They **weren't bad.***

5. delicious / terrible

_____

2. sweet / sour

_____

6. sour / ripe

_____

3. baked / fried

_____

7. long / short

_____

4. greasy / juicy

_____

8. large / small

_____

F: Follow the example.

1. breakfast

What was for breakfast?

Cereal was for breakfast.

Were there any eggs?

No, there weren't any eggs.

2. lunch

3. dinner

4. dessert

5. lunch

Exercises

G: Listen to the story and choose the correct answer.
Visit **www.basicesl.com/workbook-2/lesson-19** to listen to the story.

1. The boy wants ___*cake*___ for breakfast.

          a. cake   **b.** omelet   **c.** bacon

2. There is cereal, fruit, and _____ for breakfast.

          a. ham   **b.** pancakes   **c.** pizza

3. There were _____ apples on the table yesterday.

          a. two   **b.** three   **c.** four

4. The boy wants _____ with his pancakes.

          a. toast   **b.** shrimp   **c.** fries

5. There _____ any bread at the store.

          a. was   **b.** wasn't   **c.** is

6. Father was hungry for _____.

          a. steak   **b.** pizza   **c.** pasta

7. The boy likes _____ with his pasta.

          a. chicken   **b.** meat   **c.** shrimp

8. The boys wants _____ pie for dessert.

          a. cherry   **b.** chocolate   **c.** peach

Workbook 2

Meals

Lesson 20: Restaurant

Simple past statements with regular verbs

Spelling rules for simple past regular verbs

 basicesl.com/workbook-2/lesson-20

☐	Watch vocabulary video. Listen and repeat.
☐	Complete vocabulary exercises. (**Download**)
☐	Watch grammar video. Listen and repeat.
☐	Complete grammar exercises. (**Workbook**)
☐	Complete extra grammar exercises. (**Download**)
☐	Take a quiz. (**Download**)

Vocabulary

1. diner	**2.** bar	**3.** buffet	**4.** cafe
5. chef	**6.** bartender	**7.** server	**8.** cashier
9. menu	**10.** tray	**11.** bill	**12.** tip
13. appetizer	**14.** straw	**15.** booth	**16.** highchair
17. to taste (*verb*)	**18.** to carry (*verb*)	**19.** to order (*verb*)	**20.** to serve (*verb*)

21. great (*adj*)

22. okay (*adj*)

23. terrible (*adj, adv*)

24. ago (*adv*)

25. last (*adj, adv*)

26. to create (*verb*)

27. to place (*verb*)

28. to remove (*verb*)

29. to enjoy (*verb*)

* Irregular verb list page 6

Grammar

Simple past statements with regular verbs

enjoy → enjoy**ed**	work → work**ed**
talk → talk**ed**	order → order**ed**

Present	Past
I *enjoy* the food here.	I **enjoyed** the food here.
You *talk* to the bartender.	You **talked** to the bartender.
He *asks* the customers.	He **asked** the customers.
She *works* at the cafe.	She **worked** at the cafe.
It *melts* in the pan.	It **melted** in the pan.
We *clean* the buffet counter.	We **cleaned** the buffet counter.
You *order* the appetizers.	You **ordered** the appetizers.
They *grill* the steak.	They **grilled** the steak.

I *work* at the diner.	I **worked** at the diner last night.
You *talk* to the chef.	You **talked** to the chef this morning.
Jeff *cleans* the booths.	He **cleaned** the booths 5 minutes ago.
The bar *closes* at 2 a.m.	It **closed** at midnight yesterday.
The chef *creates* the menu.	She **created** a new menu last week.

The simple past tense is used to talk about things that happened before now. Past tense regular verbs end in -*ed*. For most verbs, add -*ed* to the base form of the verb.

> most verbs → add -**ed**

For regular verbs, the past tense form is the same for all subjects.

Singular	Plural
I **worked**	We **worked**
You **worked**	You **worked**
He **worked**	They **worked**
She **worked**	
It **worked**	

Spelling rules for past tense regular verbs

For regular verbs ending in a silent -e, remove the -*e* and add -**ed**.

slice → slic**ed**	remove → remov**ed**
taste → tast**ed**	close → clos**ed**

The bartender **sliced** the lemons.	I **removed** the tips from the table.
John **tasted** the appetizer.	The cafe **closed** an hour ago.

For verbs ending in -**y**, change the -*y* to an -*i* and add -**ed**.

carry → carr**ied**	cry → cr**ied**
fry → fr**ied**	study → stud**ied**

He **carried** the tray to the booth.	The baby **cried** in the highchair.
You **fried** the eggs for breakfast.	The servers **studied** the menu.

For single syllable verbs ending consonant + vowel + consonant (except -*w* or -*x*), double the consonant and add -**ed**.

stir → stir**red**	chop → chop**ped**
plan → plan**ned**	stop → stop**ped**

I **stirred** my milk with a straw.	We **chopped** the yellow onions.
Adam **planned** a great lunch.	He **stopped** for lunch at the buffet.

Regular verbs are verbs that end in -*ed* in the simple past tense. For most verbs, add -*ed* to the base form of the verb.

There are other spelling rules that depend on the ending of the verb.

> ends in silent -*e* → remove -*e* + -**ed**
> ends in -*y* → change -*y to -i* + -**ed**
> ends in *vowel + consonant* → double *consonant* +-**ed**

Exercises

A: Write the **simple past** tense verb form.

1. love	*loved*	**11.** finish	
2. ask		**12.** cross	
3. show		**13.** fry	
4. want		**14.** stir	
5. use		**15.** share	
6. multiply		**16.** chop	
7. look		**17.** end	
8. answer		**18.** live	
9. pick		**19.** try	
10. grab		**20.** work	

B: Write the statement in the **simple past** tense.

1. The server needs a tip. ___*The server **needed** a tip.*___

2. We carry the trays to the kitchen. _____

3. Sheila enjoys the chef's pasta. _____

4. You need an appetizer. _____

5. I like the bartender. _____

6. We remove the tips from the table. _____

7. They place the plates on the trays. _____

8. The cashier closes the diner. _____

9. You stir the drinks. _____

10. Andy and Kristen taste the food. _____

Exercises

C: Write a present and a **past** tense statement. Use the given <u>clue</u>. Follow the example.

1. to fold-Mary-napkins

 Mary folds the napkins.

 <u>this morning</u>

 *She **folded** the napkins <u>this morning.</u>*

2. to be-restaurant-closed

 _____

 two weeks ago

 _____

3. to serve-I-appetizers

 _____

 last night

 _____

4. to prepare-bartender-drinks

 _____

 for the customers

 _____

5. to chop-Katy and I-onions

 _____

 first

 _____

6. to use-chefs-ripe vegetables

 _____

 last week

 _____

D: Complete the **past** tense statement. Use each verb once.

1. The chef ___*grilled*___ the steaks on the kitchen grill.

2. My parents _____ a tasty lunch at the new diner.

3. I _____ the tray back to the kitchen.

4. She _____ the bill from the table.

5. The customers _____ from the menu.

6. The downtown cafe _____ last year.

7. The appetizers _____ terrible.

8. The mother _____ the cake with a knife.

9. The server_____ questions about the menu.

10. Alan _____ a lot of salt on his eggs.

to carry

to order

to slice

to taste

to grill

to answer

to grab

to sprinkle

to close

to enjoy

Exercises

E: Rewrite the story in the **past** tense.

I work at the diner on Tuesday night. Tuesday is a good night at the diner. The chef serves appetizers to the cashiers and the servers. We enjoy shrimp, fish and many tasty fruits.

For work I remove the dirty plates from the tables. I place clean forks and napkins for new customers. I clean the trays for the servers. I wash the cups and glasses for the bartender.

I help the chef at 11:00 p.m. because the Cherry Diner closes at midnight. The chefs clean the grill, oven, counters and the kitchen floor. The bartenders return the menus to the bar. I stay after 12 p.m. on Tuesday night.

I **worked** ...

Exercises

F: Follow the example.

1. <u>you</u> / this morning / to order

Where were <u>you</u> this morning?

*I **was** at the cafe.*

*I **ordered** a coffee.*

2. Tom / at lunch / to try

_____

_____

3. friends / on Friday / to enjoy

_____

_____

_____

4. I / on Monday / to clean

_____

_____

_____

5. servers / yesterday / to create

_____

_____

_____

Exercises

G: Listen to the story and choose the correct answer.
Visit **www.basicesl.com/workbook-2/lesson-20** to listen to the story.

1. Tony's family tried a new cafe by the _post office_ .

        a. post office   **b.** church   **c.** buffet

2. The cafe opened last _____ .

        a. week   **b.** month   **c.** year

3. The cafe was _____ .

        a. clean   **b.** dirty   **c.** ugly

4. The server showed the family to a big _____ .

        a. booth   **b.** highchair   **c.** table

5. The server _____ coffee for Tony's parents.

        a. ordered   **b.** placed   **c.** poured

6. The _____ offered some bread.

        a. bartender   **b.** cashier   **c.** chef

7. Tony ordered _____ and bacon.

        a. eggs   **b.** pancakes   **c.** omelet

8. Tony's family _____ the new cafe.

        a. enjoyed   **b.** created   **c.** worked

Workbook 2
Meals
Lesson 21: Grocery Store

Past tense negative statements

Past tense questions

Irregular verbs in the past tense

 basicesl.com/workbook-2/lesson-21

☐ Watch vocabulary video. Listen and repeat.

☐ Complete vocabulary exercises. (**Download**)

☐ Watch grammar video. Listen and repeat.

☐ Complete grammar exercises. (**Workbook**)

☐ Complete extra grammar exercises. (**Download**)

☐ Take a quiz. (**Download**)

Vocabulary

1. can	2. jar	3. box	4. bag
5. bottle	6. salad dressing	7. oil	8. vinegar
9. mustard	10. ketchup	11. soda	12. yogurt
13. candy	14. cookie	15. chips	16. nuts
17. basket	18. cart	19. coupon	20. list

21. snack (*noun*)   22. plastic (*noun*)   23. glass (*noun*)

24. trash (*noun*)   25. container (*noun*)   26. to squirt (*verb*)

27. to push (*verb*)   28. to pull (*verb*)   29. to load (*verb*)

Irregular verb list page 6

Grammar

Past tense irregular verbs *to be, to do, to have* and *to go*

to be → **was, were**	*to have* → **had**
to do → **did**	*to go* → **went**

Present	Past
I *am* thirsty.	I **was** thirsty.
You *are* hungry.	You **were** hungry.
He *does* the shopping.	He **did** the shopping.
We *have* a coupon.	We **had** a coupon.
They *go* to the store every day.	They **went** to the store yesterday.

Past tense regular verbs end in *-ed*. Past tense irregular verbs do not end in *-ed*. Irregular verbs like *to be, to do, to have* and *to go* have different forms in the past tense.

* *Irregular verb list page 6*

Simple past negative statements

Statement	Negative statement
I *opened* the can of beans.	I **did not open** the can of beans.
You *asked* for a bag of chips.	You **didn't ask** for a bag of chips.
He *mixed* the nuts and yogurt.	He **did not mix** the nuts and yogurt.
She *grabbed* the candy jar.	She **didn't grab** the candy jar.
It *squirted* on his shirt.	It **did not squirt** on his shirt.
We *needed* a lot of vinegar.	We **didn't need** a lot of vinegar.
You *pulled* the door open.	You **did not pull** the door open.
They *carried* their basket.	They **didn't carry** their basket.

Negative past tense statements use the words *did not* before the **base** form of the main verb. The base form of the main verb is used for all subjects.

Subject + **did not** + **base verb**

The contraction of the words *did* and *not* is *didn't*.

did not → **didn't**

Simple past tense questions

Statement	Question
I *spilled* your soda.	**Did** I **spill** your soda?
You *used* a coupon.	**Did** you **use** a coupon?
He *loaded* a basket with snacks.	**Did** he **load** a basket with snacks?
She *pushed* the cart.	**Did** she **push** the cart?
It *melted* in the bag.	**Did** it **melt** in the bag?
We *placed* the box in the trash.	**Did** we **place** the box in the trash?
You *shared* your candy.	**Did** you **share** your candy?
They *opened* the bottle of oil.	**Did** they **open** the bottle of oil?

Past tense questions begin with the word *did* followed by the subject. The **base** form of the verb is used for all subjects.

Did + subject + **base verb**

We use *yes* and *no* to answer questions, followed by a comma and a statement.

Short answers are formed with the subject and the words *did* or *did not*.

Question	Answer
Did you **need** the basket?	**No, I didn't need** the basket.
What did you **need**?	I **needed** the **cart**.
Did Sam **push** the cart?	**Yes**, he **pushed** the cart.
Where did Sam **push** the cart?	He **pushed** the cart **in the store**.
Did you **shop** for food today?	**Yes, I did**.
When did you **shop**?	I **shopped this morning**.
Did Tim **ask** Lisa for the list?	**No**, he **didn't**.
Who did he **ask**?	Tim **asked Nicki** for the list.

Exercises

A: Form the beginning of **simple past sentences**. Use the given pronoun and verb. Follow the example.

	Simple past	Negative simple past	Simple past question
1. they / want	*They wanted*	*They did not want*	*Did they want*
2. I / push			
3. you / go			
4. we / pull			
5. he / open			
6. she / have			
7. you / ask			
8. they / need			
9. we / carry			
10. I / shop			

B: Write the question for the given answer.

1. ___**Did** Mary **want** the mustard?___   **Yes**, Mary **wanted** the mustard.

2. _____ No, Alan didn't shop with a cart.

3. _____ Yes, they tasted the yogurt.

4. _____ No, I did not prepare the salad dressing.

5. _____ Yes, we shared the nuts.

6. _____ No, they didn't move the soda.

7. _____ Yes, Alice spilled the vinegar.

8. _____ Yes, Henry cleaned the jars.

9. _____ No, you did not use the right glass.

10. _____ Yes, I finished the candy.

C: Write a simple past question and answers using the given **clues**. Follow the example.

1. John / to go / store

today, yesterday

*Did John go to the store **today**?*

*No, he didn't go to the store **today**.*

*He went to the store **yesterday**.*

2. Ana / to use / coupon

yesterday, this morning

3. Mark / to have / candy

last week, yesterday

4. you / to open / box

today, 5 minutes ago

5. they / to bake / cookies

on Saturday , yesterday

6. Seth / to wash / bottles

last Monday, this afternoon

7. I / to do / it

before noon, after 3 p.m.

Exercises

D: Read the story. Answer each question with a complete sentence. Use subject pronouns.

My name is Olivia. My husband and I shopped for groceries on Sunday. We went to Savers Grocery Store near our house. My husband pushed the cart through the store. There were not many things on our list. From our list I added a bottle of salad dressing, a bottle of vinegar and some ketchup to our cart. I also added six plastic containers of cherry yogurt. My husband grabbed a box of cookies on aisle six and added them to the cart. The cookies were not on the list. We walked to the front of the store. There wasn't an open register. We waited in line for 10 minutes. We talked with a nice customer and her two children in line. We paid the cashier for our food.

1. When did <u>Olivia and her husband</u> shop for groceries?

They shopped for groceries **on Sunday.**

_____

2. Where did Olivia and her husband go?

_____

_____

3. Did Olivia's husband **push** the cart through the store?

_____

_____

4. What did Olivia's husband grab on aisle six?

_____

_____

5. Was there an open register?

_____

_____

6. How long did Olivia and her husband wait in line?

_____

_____

7. Who did Olivia pay for their food?

_____

_____

E: Follow the example.

1. you / to open

Did you open the yogurt?

No, I didn't open the yogurt.

What did you open?

I opened the nuts.

2. Robert / to grill

3. Sheila / to taste

4. Tim and Pam / to enjoy

5. I / to order

Exercises

F: Write the question for the given answer.

1. _____*What* did Tom have?_____   Tom had **some chips.**

2. _____   Ann went **to the park.**

3. _____   **We** did the cooking.

4. _____   Karen was **at work** yesterday.

5. _____   I was with **my brother.**

6. _____   **Yes,** they **had** a coupon.

7. _____   David went with **Tom.**

8. _____   **Yes,** I **did** it.

9. _____   I was there **this morning.**

10. _____   **Yes,** I **had** a cookie.

G: Listen to the story and choose the correct answer.
Visit **www.basicesl.com/workbook-2/lesson-21** to listen to the story.

1. Emily and Ally went to the diner for _____ .   **a.** breakfast   **(b.)** lunch   **c.** dinner

2. There were _____ people in the diner.   **a.** no   **b.** a few   **c.** a lot of

3. Emily and Ally's booth was near _____ .   **a.** a door   **b.** the kitchen   **c.** a window

4. Emily and Ally ordered _____ to drink.   **a.** coffee   **b.** oil   **c.** soda

5. Emily ordered a hamburger and _____ .   **a.** chips   **b.** nuts   **c.** a salad

6. She wanted salad dressing in a small _____ .   **a.** container   **b.** cup   **c.** jar

7. Ally ordered _____ .   **a.** chicken   **b.** nuts   **c.** soup

8. Emily squirted _____ on her hamburger.   **a.** ketchup   **b.** mustard   **c.** dressing

Workbook 2
Measurements
Lesson 22: Length, Width & Depth

Pronunciation of *-ed* with past tense verbs

Questions about measurement

 basicesl.com/workbook-2/lesson-22

☐ Watch vocabulary video. Listen and repeat.

☐ Complete vocabulary exercises. (**Download**)

☐ Watch grammar video. Listen and repeat.

☐ Complete grammar exercises. (**Workbook**)

☐ Complete extra grammar exercises. (**Download**)

☐ Take a quiz. (**Download**)

Vocabulary

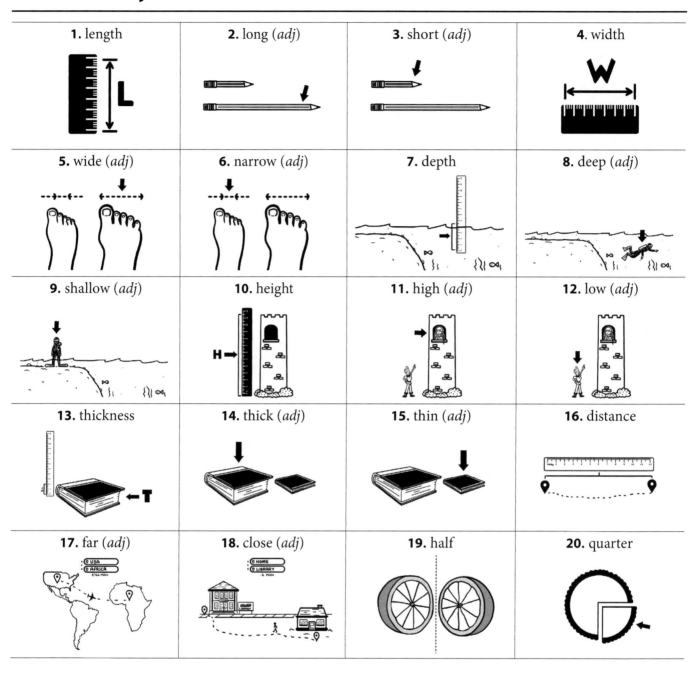

1. length

2. long (*adj*)

3. short (*adj*)

4. width

5. wide (*adj*)

6. narrow (*adj*)

7. depth

8. deep (*adj*)

9. shallow (*adj*)

10. height

11. high (*adj*)

12. low (*adj*)

13. thickness

14. thick (*adj*)

15. thin (*adj*)

16. distance

17. far (*adj*)

18. close (*adj*)

19. half

20. quarter

21. very (*adv*)

22. about (*adv*)

23. away (*adv*)

24. to fit (*verb**)

25. to guess (*verb*)

26. to bring (*verb**)

27. to set (*verb**)

28. to compare (*verb*)

29. to measure (*verb*)

* Irregular verb list page 6

Pronunciation of -ed with simple past verbs

If the base form ends in a sound like /d/ or /t/, the -ed is **pronounced /id/**.

need → nee**d**ed [need/**id**/]
add → ad**d**ed [add/**id**/]

The chef need**ed** a long knife.
I add**ed** a lot of salt to the soup.

melt → mel**t**ed [melt/**id**/]
taste → tas**t**ed [taste/**id**/]

You melt**ed** a thick piece of cheese.
We tast**ed** some different fruits.

If the base form ends in a sound like /f/, /k/, /p/, /s/, /x/, /ch/, or /sh/, the -ed is **pronounced /t/**.

guess → gues**s**ed [guess/**t**/]
push → pu**sh**ed [push/**t**/]

Bob guess**ed** the wrong distance.
Jared push**ed** the cart far away.

help → hel**p**ed [help/**t**/]
look → loo**k**ed [look/**t**/]

Stacy help**ed** for a very short time.
Alice look**ed** low under the table.

For all other past tense verbs, the -ed is **pronounced /d/**.

mo**v**e → mo**v**ed [move/**d**/]
grab → gra**bb**ed [grab/**d**/]

Bob and Sue mov**ed** close by.
The girl grabb**ed** a thin sweater.

play → pla**y**ed [play/**d**/]
measure → measu**r**ed [measure/**d**/]

The boy play**ed** in the shallow water.
She measur**ed** the width of the table.

Simple past tense verbs end in -ed. The pronunciation of -ed is different for different verbs. It depends on what the ending of the base form of the verb sounds like.

There are three ways to pronounce -ed for simple past tense verbs.

/id/: nee**d**ed [need/**id**/]
/t/: gues**s**ed [guess/**t**/]
/d/: mo**v**ed [move/**d**/]

Questions about measurement

What is the **length** of the table?
How **long** is the table?

The **length** is **8 feet**.
The table is **8 feet long**.

What is the **width** of the door?
How **wide** is the door?

The **width** is **32 inches**.
The door is **32 inches wide**.

What is the **depth** of the lake?
How **deep** is the lake?

The **depth** is about **15 meters**.
The lake is about **15 meters deep**.

What is the **thickness** of the book?
How **thick** is the book?

The **thickness** is **half an inch**.
The book is **half an inch thick**.

What is the **distance** to my house?
How **far** is my house?

The **distance** is **3 miles**.
Your house is **3 miles away**.

Questions about measurement are asked with the question words *what* or *how*.

What + to be + **noun**... ?
How + **adjective** + to be... ?

Measurement Abbreviations

mile → mi.
foot → ft.
inch → in.

kilometer → km.
meter → m.
centimeter → cm.

Exercises

A: Write the **opposite** adjective.

1. low _____high_____

2. tall _____

3. close _____

4. deep _____

5. long _____

6. narrow _____

7. thick _____

8. hard _____

9. huge _____

10. young _____

B: Write the **simple past** tense form of the verb.

1. to go _____went_____

2. to have _____

3. to eat _____

4. to burn _____

5. to fix _____

6. to drink _____

7. to taste _____

8. to come _____

9. to need _____

10. to make _____

C: Choose the correct **pronunciation** of **-ed** for the given past tense verb.

Sounds Like:	't'	'id'	'd'		't'	'id'	'd'
1. helped	X	____	____	11. added	____	____	____
2. switched	____	____	____	12. stopped	____	____	____
3. burned	____	____	____	13. fixed	____	____	____
4. shared	____	____	____	14. peeled	____	____	____
5. needed	____	____	____	15. pushed	____	____	____
6. moved	____	____	____	16. grabbed	____	____	____
7. placed	____	____	____	17. hugged	____	____	____
8. tasted	____	____	____	18. suggested	____	____	____
9. mixed	____	____	____	19. cooked	____	____	____
10. measured	____	____	____	20. compared	____	____	____

D: Write two measurement questions for the given statement using how and what. Follow the example.

1. The table is three feet long.

 How long is the table?

 What is the length of the table?

2. The desk is 36 inches wide.

3. Henry is five feet four inches tall.

4. The river is two feet deep.

5. The flag is thirty feet high.

6. The book is half an inch thick.

7. The church is 5 miles away.

E: Correct the **simple past** tense verb form and the <u>underlined</u> words.

1. I **puted** the fruit <u>in the table</u>.

 *I **put** the fruit **on the table**.*

2. He **maked** eggs <u>the lunch</u>.

3. He **eated** <u>to me</u> yesterday.

4. I **cutted** the straw <u>at half</u>.

5. She **drived** <u>for long</u> way.

6. She **bringed** <u>an thick</u> book.

7. We **drinked** <u>a lot tea</u>.

8. It **comed** <u>close me</u>.

Exercises

F: Change the **verbs** to the past tense. Use an opposite for the underlined <u>adjective</u>. Fill in the blanks with: *length, distance, thickness* or *depth*.

Steve **loves** his <u>new</u> house at the lake. The lake **is** <u>far from</u> his house. The _____ from the house to the lake **is** about 500 feet.

Steve's uncle **measures** the _____ of the lake every summer. The lake **is** very <u>shallow</u> in July.

Steve **makes** tables and chairs for his lake house. Two of the tables **are** 10 feet <u>wide</u>. Steve **set** the _____ of the tables to 10 feet because he **has** a <u>small</u> family. The table tops **are** very <u>thin</u>. The _____ **is** about two inches.

Steve and his uncle **eat** lunch every day on the <u>inside</u> patio. They **take** their sandwiches and snacks to the <u>east</u> patio. Steve's uncle **cuts** the sandwiches into quarters.

*Steve **loved** his <u>old</u> house at the lake.*

_____

_____

_____

_____

_____

_____

_____

_____

_____

_____

_____

_____

_____

_____

_____

_____

_____

G: Follow the example. Use contractions.

1. to measure / width / 48 in.

narrow

I measured the door.

*How **wide** is the door?*

*The **width** is forty-eight inches.*

*It isn't **narrow**.*

2. to visit / length / 2 km.

short

3. to stop / depth / 26 ft.

shallow

4. to bring / thickness / 4 in.

thin

5. to go / distance / 20 miles

close

Exercises

H: Listen to the audio and write the verb. Choose the correct pronunciation of *-ed*.
Visit **www.basicesl.com/workbook-2/lesson-22** to listen to the audio.

1. *needed*   **(a.)** /id/   **b.** /d/   **c.** /t/

2. _____   **a.** /id/   **b.** /d/   **c.** /t/

3. _____   **a.** /id/   **b.** /d/   **c.** /t/

4. _____   **a.** /id/   **b.** /d/   **c.** /t/

5. _____   **a.** /id/   **b.** /d/   **c.** /t/

6. _____   **a.** /id/   **b.** /d/   **c.** /t/

7. _____   **a.** /id/   **b.** /d/   **c.** /t/

8. _____   **a.** /id/   **b.** /d/   **c.** /t/

9. _____   **a.** /id/   **b.** /d/   **c.** /t/

10. _____   **a.** /id/   **b.** /d/   **c.** /t/

I: Listen to the story and choose the correct answer.
Visit **www.basicesl.com/workbook-2/lesson-22** to listen to the story.

1. Jacob has shelves in his bedroom _____ .   **a.** counter   **(b.)** closet   **c.** cupboard

2. The low shelf is three feet from the _____ .   **a.** ceiling   **b.** floor   **c.** high shelf

3. The shelves are five feet _____ .   **a.** long   **b.** wide   **c.** deep

4. The _____ of each shelf is about 1 inch.   **a.** height   **b.** length   **c.** thickness

5. Jacob is buying new _____ from the store.   **a.** shelves   **b.** lamps   **c.** closets

6. Jacob _____ to the store.   **a.** drove   **b.** drived   **c.** walked

7. The store is about 2 _____ away.   **a.** kilometers   **b.** inches   **c.** miles

8. Jacob put the _____ shelves in his cart.   **a.** cheap   **b.** expensive   **c.** used

Workbook 2
Measurements
Lesson 23: Weight

Past continuous statements and questions

Using *when* and *while*

Questions about weight

 basicesl.com/workbook-2/lesson-23

- [ ] Watch vocabulary video. Listen and repeat.
- [ ] Complete vocabulary exercises. (**Download**)
- [ ] Watch grammar video. Listen and repeat.
- [ ] Complete grammar exercises. (**Workbook**)
- [ ] Complete extra grammar exercises. (**Download**)
- [ ] Take a quiz. (**Download**)

Vocabulary

1. liquid	2. measuring cup	3. weight	4. scale
5. full (*adj*)	6. empty (*adj*)	7. heavy (*adj*)	8. light (*adj*)
5. *5* gallon *bottle*	6. *2* liter *bottle*	7. *45* pound *weight*	8. *100* gram *apple*
13. bucket	14. mop	15. broom	16. dustpan
17. sponge	18. cleaner	19. duster	20. vacuum

21. to fill (*verb*)   **22.** to empty (*verb*)   **23.** to change (*verb*)

24. to wipe (*verb*)   **25.** to sweep (*verb**)   **26.** to scrub (*verb*)

27. to lift (*verb*)   **28.** to drop (*verb*)   **29.** to weigh (*verb*)

* Irregular verb list page 6

Grammar

Past continuous statements and questions

Present continuous
I *am* **emptying** the 12 ounce cans.
He *is* **filling** a 2 liter bottle.
They *are* **weighing** heavy boxes.
We *are* **scrubbing** the dirty sink.

Past continuous
I **was emptying** the 12 ounce cans.
He **was filling** a 2 liter bottle.
They **were weighing** heavy boxes.
We **were scrubbing** the dirty sink.

Statement
I **was mopping** in the kitchen.
She **was mixing** two liquids.
You **were lifting** 100 pounds.
They **were using** a new cleaner.

Negative statement
I **was** not **mopping** in the kitchen.
She **wasn't mixing** two liquids.
You **were** not **lifting** 100 pounds.
They **weren't using** a new cleaner.

Statement
John **was drinking** water.
The liquid **was changing** color.
You **were cleaning** with a sponge.
They **were guessing** my weight.

Question
Was John **drinking** water?
Was the liquid **changing** color?
Were you **cleaning** with a sponge?
Were they **guessing** my weight?

The past continuous tense expresses an ongoing action that happened in the past. It is formed with the past tense form of the verb *to be* and the present participle (*-ing* form) of the main verb.

am walking → **was walking**
are walking → **were walking**
is walking → **was walking**

The word *not* after the verb *to be* is used to make negative statements. Contractions are made with the verb *to be* and the word *not*.

was *not* → **wasn't**
were *not* → **weren't**

Using *when* and *while*

John dropped a full bucket. • He **fell** down the stairs.
John dropped a full bucket **when** he **fell** down the stairs.

I left the house. • Jeff and Sally **were cleaning**.
I left the house **while** Jeff and Sally **were cleaning**.

John was lifting heavy weights. • Jane **walked** in.
John was lifting heavy weights **when** Jane **walked** in.

Kim was wiping the counter. • You **were talking**.
Kim was wiping the counter **while** you **were talking**.

What was Ruby doing **when** Reggie **came** over?
She was vacuuming upstairs.

What did Fred do **while** Sam **was cleaning** downstairs?
He swept the kitchen floor.

It is common to use the words *when* and *while* with the past continuous tense. These words are used to express a relationship between two past events.

We use *when* with the past simple tense. We use *while* with the past continuous tense.

when + past simple
while + past continuous

Questions about weight

How much do you **weigh?**   I weigh **155 pounds**.
How much does an apple **weigh?** It weighs about **100 grams**.
How much does water **weigh?**   16 ounces of water weighs **1 pound**.

Weight and liquid measurements
gallon → gal.   pound → lb.   ounce → oz.
liter → l.   kilogram → kg.   gram → g.

Questions about weight use the question words *how much* and the verb *to weigh*.

Exercises

A: Write the measurement noun related to the given word.

1. tall _height_
2. narrow _____
3. low _____
4. shallow _____
5. west _____
6. far _____
7. meter _____
8. heavy _____
9. deep _____
10. long _____

11. mile _____
12. light _____
13. gallon _____
14. small _____
15. pound _____
16. high _____
17. gram _____
18. inch _____
19. medium _____
20. short _____

B: Write the **past continuous** form for the given subject and verb. Follow the example

	Statement	Negative statement	Question
1. he / to run	_He was running_	_He was not running_	_Was he running_
2. they / to fill	_____	_____	_____
3. she / to empty	_____	_____	_____
4. we / to drop	_____	_____	_____
5. it / to change	_____	_____	_____
6. you / to push	_____	_____	_____
7. they / to pull	_____	_____	_____
8. I / to be	_____	_____	_____
9. he / to scrub	_____	_____	_____
10. we / to try	_____	_____	_____

Exercises

C: Use the given clues to write a **simple past** and a **past continuous** sentence. Follow the example.

1. Sally / to wipe (not) / mirror / water

Sally **didn't wipe** the mirror with water.

Sally / to wipe / mirror / cleaner

Sally **was wiping** the mirror with a cleaner.

2. Greg / to put / vacuum / away

Greg / to put (not) / vacuum / closet

3. Gina / to scrub / sink / sponge

Gina / to scrub (not) / toilet / hand

4. The girls / to use / duster / blinds

The boys / to use / mop / floor

5. You / to take / dustpan / garage

You / to take (not) / bucket / outside

6. I / to sweep / garage / broom

I / to sweep / floor / noon

D: Change the simple past question to a **past continuous** question.

1. Did he fill the buckets?

Was he filling the buckets?

2. Did she move the carts?

3. Did they get the 2 liter bottle?

4. Did it work?

5. Did you use heavy weights?

6. Did they empty the gallon buckets?

7. Did Tom visit his mother?

8. Did you teach math?

9. Did Bill and Sharon run fast?

10. Did you look for the can?

Exercises

1. you / to move

| 42 lb. |

What were you moving?

I was moving a 5-gallon bottle.

How much did the bottle weigh?

It weighed 42 pounds.

2. John / to fill

| 10 lb. |

3. the boys / to weigh

| 9 kg. |

4. you / to buy

| 140 lb. |

5. Mom / to get

| 1 oz. |

Exercises

F: Complete the sentences. Use **while** with the **past continuous**. Use **when** with the **simple past**.

1. I was having breakfast _____ *when* _____ Alan *arrived* from the store.

2. Alan put away the dishes _____ I was eating.

3. Reggie hurt his back _____ he lifted the heavy weight.

4. Was Jenny with her brother _____ you talked to her?

5. My sister peeled carrots _____ we were chopping the onions.

6. My brother drank a pint of milk _____ we were standing in line.

7. I lifted a lot of weight _____ I carried the boxes to the scale.

8. A customer asked for you _____ you were emptying the trash outside.

9. We did plenty of homework _____ our mom was changing sheets.

10. The customers were waiting _____ Bill arrived at the store.

G: Complete the sentences. Use the **past continuous** tense with **while**. Use the **simple past** with **when**.

1. I was lifting the full bucket *when* Alan **(to drop)** _____ *dropped* _____ an empty box.

2. My sister left for work *while* I **(to prepare)** _____ dinner last night.

3. I was washing the dishes *when* my brother **(to spill)** _____ the milk.

4. My father slept on the couch *while* my Mom and I **(to bake)** _____ a cake.

5. I was lifting weights *when* Henry **(to tell)** _____ Betty about the party.

6. Boris wasn't wearing shoes *when* he **(to come)** _____ into the kitchen.

7. Michael did his homework *while* Morgan **(to watch)** _____ TV.

8. I went to the restroom *while* my sister **(to pay)** _____ for the coat.

9. Gary listened to music *while* he **(to do)** _____ his homework.

10. I didn't have an answer *when* my father **(to ask)** _____ the question.

Exercises

H: Listen to the story and choose the correct answer.
Visit **www.basicesl.com/workbook-2/lesson-23** to listen to the story.

1. Henry helped his ___*aunt*___ make sauce.

           a. aunt   **b.** grandmother   **c.** sister

2. What size containers were used for the sauce?

           a. liter   **b.** pint   **c.** quart

3. The tomatoes on the patio were in _____ .

           a. buckets   **b.** boxes   **c.** quarts

4. How much did the bucket weigh?

           a. 10 lb.   **b.** 20 lb.   **c.** 30 lb.

5. Henry _____ the tomatoes into the sink.

           a. acted   **b.** filled   **c.** emptied

6. Henry's aunt _____ the onions for the sauce.

           a. cut   **b.** cutted   **c.** chopped

7. Henry's aunt weighed 4 _____ of tomatoes.

           a. ounces   **b.** pounds   **c.** grams

8. What time did they cut the tomatoes?

           a. noon   **b.** at 12:30   **c.** lunch time

Workbook 2

Measurements

Lesson 24: Tools

Object pronouns

Possessive pronouns

 basicesl.com/workbook-2/lesson-24

- ☐ Watch vocabulary video. Listen and repeat.
- ☐ Complete vocabulary exercises. (**Download**)
- ☐ Watch grammar video. Listen and repeat.
- ☐ Complete grammar exercises. (**Workbook**)
- ☐ Complete extra grammar exercises. (**Download**)
- ☐ Take a quiz. (**Download**)

Vocabulary

1. tool	**2.** ladder	**3.** hammer	**4.** nail
5. screwdriver	**6.** screw	**7.** wood	**8.** metal
9. wrench	**10.** pliers	**11.** bolt	**12.** nut
13. saw	**14.** electric saw	**15.** power drill	**16.** razor blade
17. string	**18.** rope	**19.** plug	**20.** outlet

21. electric (*adj*)

22. power (*noun*)

23. to hit (*verb**)

24. to hang (*verb**)

25. to bend (*verb**)

26. to tear (*verb**)

27. to break (*verb**)

28. to fix (*verb*)

29. to build (*verb**)

* Irregular verb list page 6

Object pronouns

Object	Object pronoun
I know *Mary*.	Mary knows **me**.
You know *Tom*.	Tom knows **you**.
He works with *Mary*.	He works with **her**.
She works with *Tom*.	She works with **him**.
Tom works with *that hammer*.	Tom works with **it**.
You remem*ber Tom and me*.	You remember **us**.
They remember *you and Mary*.	They remember **you**.
We remember *Tom and Mary*.	We remember **them**.

Question	Answer
What did Jeff make **you**?	He made **me** a new chair.
What did Ashley fix for **me**?	She fixed the window for **you**.
Are the nuts and bolts for *Tim*?	No, they aren't for **him**.
When did Bob buy *rope* for *Ann*?	He bought **it** for **her** yesterday.
Are the nails inside the *box*?	No, they're not inside **it**.
Did you leave **us** any tools?	Yes, we left **you** plenty of tools.
Was John with **you** *and Brian*?	Yes, he was with **us**.
Did you build the chair for *the girls*?	Yes, we built **it** for **them**.

Object pronouns replace object nouns. A noun receiving the action in a sentence is an object noun.

Subject → **Object**

I → **me**	we → **us**
you → **you**	you → **you**
he → **him**	they → **them**
she → **her**	
it → **it**	

Possessive pronouns

Possessive adjective + noun	Possessive pronoun
That electric saw is *my saw*.	That electric saw is **mine**.
This metal ladder is *your ladder*.	This metal ladder is **yours**.
The long hammer is *his hammer*.	The long hammer is **his**.
Those power tools are *her tools*.	Those power tools are **hers**.
These wood screws are *our screws*.	These wood screws are **ours**.
The thin pliers are *their pliers*.	The thin pliers are **theirs**.

Question	Answer
Whose string is that?	That is *my string*.
	That is **mine**.
Whose screwdrivers are these?	Those are *our screwdrivers*.
	Those are **ours**.
Is that 6 foot ladder **ours**?	Yes, it's *your ladder*.
	Yes, it's **yours**.
Are those half inch wrenches **hers**?	No, those aren't *her wrenches*.
	No, those aren't **hers**.

Possessive pronouns refer to nouns that belong to someone. Possessive pronouns replace nouns or noun phrases that show possession.

Possessive Adjective	→	**Possessive Pronoun**
my → **mine**		our → **ours**
your → **yours**		your → **yours**
his → **his**		their → **theirs**
her → **hers**		
it → **its**		

Exercises

A: Write the **object pronoun** and **possessive pronoun** for the given subject.

1. he _him_____ _his_____

2. she _____ _____

3. I _____ _____

4. you _____ _____

5. we _____ _____

6. they _____ _____

7. you and I _____ _____

8. he and she _____ _____

9. the men _____ _____

10. the women _____ _____

11. the family _____ _____

12. Jane _____ _____

13. John _____ _____

14. you and her _____ _____

15. it _____ _____

16. the school _____ _____

B: Write the correct **object pronoun** for the underlined word or words.

1. John is building a <u>house</u> for Ann. He is building ___it_____ with his new tools.

2. Frank fixed <u>Ed</u>'s electric saw. He fixed it for _____ last week.

3. <u>I</u> know Mary. She helped _____ with my electric problem.

4. I know <u>Mary</u>. I helped _____ when she was fixing her outlets.

5. <u>John and I</u> wanted to use nails. Albert told _____ to use screws.

6. <u>John and Albert</u> fix refrigerators. I asked _____ about my refrigerator.

7. I use my <u>saw</u> to cut wood. I use _____ every day.

8. <u>You</u> bent the metal with your hammer. I watched _____ while you were bending it.

9. <u>Martin</u> likes his new <u>electric drill</u>. I bought _____ for _____ yesterday.

10. <u>Samantha</u> is hanging a picture in the living room. Take _____ a ladder.

11. The teacher asked <u>Randy</u> to hold the rope. She thanked _____ for his help.

12. The boys didn't break the saw. I asked _____ to be serious.

Exercises

C: Complete the sentences with the correct **object** and **possessive** pronouns. Follow the example.

1. **I** love this wrench.

This wrench is __*mine*__.

Bob gave the wrench to __*me*__.

2. **We** build with these tools.

These tools are _____.

Dad gave the tools to_____.

3. This **electric saw** is dirty.

There is oil on _____ plug.

I need to wash _____.

4. **John and Steve** have a red ladder.

This blue ladder is not _____.

Ann gave _____ the red ladder.

5. **Melissa** needs a razor blade.

Is this razor blade _____?

Yes, I saw _____ with it.

6. **You** have pliers.

These pliers are _____.

Bob gave them to _____.

7. **Robert** has nuts, bolts and screws.

The nails are _____ too.

I asked _____ for two screws.

8. **Dave and I** have ten feet of rope.

The rope is _____.

Bob gave it to _____.

D: Answer the question with *yes* answers. Use **pronouns** instead of <u>nouns</u>.

1. Was <u>the hammer</u> <u>Jill's hammer</u>?

__*Yes, **it** was **hers**.*__

Did <u>Jill</u> give <u>the hammer</u> to <u>John</u>?

__*Yes, **she** gave **it** to **him**.*__

2. Was the saw John's saw?

_____

Did John give the saw to Ann?

_____

3. Were the pliers Dave's pliers?

_____

Did Dave give the pliers to Matt?

_____

4. Were the tools the boys' tools?

_____

Did the boys give the tools to Alan?

_____

5. Was the wrench Amy's wrench?

_____

Did Amy give the wrench to Daisy?

_____

Exercises

E: Rewrite the story. Use the **past tense** or **past continuous** tense for the verb forms. Replace the underlined words with **object pronouns**.

John **(to buy)** a new power drill yesterday morning. He **(to get)** the power drill at a store downtown. John **(to talk)** with his friend Dan *while* he **(to shop)**. John **(to tell)** his friend Dan about different types of tools.

This morning John **(to hang)** new kitchen cabinet doors for his wife Mary. Mary **(to leave)** the kitchen *while* John **(to tear)** the old cabinet doors out. In the afternoon he **(to fix)** a bathroom outlet for Mary.

John's daughters **(to bend)** a piece of metal on their dresser. In the evening, John **(to work)** on the dresser for his two daughters. He **(to build)** a new drawer for the dresser.

*John **bought** a new power drill yesterday morning.*

F: Follow the example. Use contractions.

1. Bob / to find / Lisa

Did Bob find a hammer for **Lisa**?

Yes, he found a hammer for **her**.

Whose hammer is it?

It's his.

2. you / to get / Phil

3. you and I / to leave / boys

4. I / to bring / you

5. Sam and Kelly / to have / metal

Exercises

G: Listen to the story and choose the correct answer.
Visit **www.basicesl.com/workbook-2/lesson-24** to listen to the story.

1. Dan is Chris's _brother_ .

        a. father   **b.** son   **c.** brother

2. They keep their _____ in the garage.

        a. buckets   **b.** tools   **c.** shelves

3. They build tables, chairs, beds and _____ .

        a. clocks   **b.** couches   **c.** ladders

4. The power drill and electric _____ are Dan's.

        a. outlet   **b.** saw   **c.** plug

5. The wrenches and _____ are Chris's.

        a. bolts   **b.** rope   **c.** pliers

6. Dan _____ Chris a wrench last week.

        a. brought   **b.** bought   **c.** got

7. They keep _____ in little jars.

        a. string   **b.** razor blades   **c.** nails

8. They keep the _____ on the shelves in the back.

        a. metal   **b.** rope   **c.** wood

Workbook 2
Animals
Lesson 25: Pets
Comparative adjectives

 basicesl.com/workbook-2/lesson-25

- ☐ Watch vocabulary video. Listen and repeat.
- ☐ Complete vocabulary exercises. (**Download**)
- ☐ Watch grammar video. Listen and repeat.
- ☐ Complete grammar exercises. (**Workbook**)
- ☐ Complete extra grammar exercises. (**Download**)
- ☐ Take a quiz. (**Download**)

Vocabulary

1. pet	**2.** fur	**3.** tail	**4.** paw
5. cat	**6.** kitten	**7.** dog	**8.** puppy
9. bird	**10.** feather	**11.** wing	**12.** beak
13. chicken	**14.** rooster	**15.** pig	**16.** cow
17. sheep	**18.** donkey	**19.** horse	**20.** hoof

21. quiet (*adj*)   **22.** loud (*adj*)   **23.** cute (*adj*)

24. lazy (*adj*)   **25.** kind (*adj*)   **26.** quick (*adj*)

27. popular (*adj*)   **28.** common (*adj*)   **29.** careful (*adj*)

Irregular verb list page 6

Grammar

Comparative adjectives

For most adjectives, add *-er.*

soft → soft**er**	hard → hard**er**
short → short**er**	tall → tall**er**
The cat's fur is *soft*.	The cat's fur is **softer** than the dog's.
John's dog is *tall*.	John's dog is **taller** than Mike's dog.

For adjectives that end in a silent *-e*, remove the *-e* and add *-er.*

nice → nic**er**	cute → cut**er**
large → larg**er**	close → clos**er**
Dogs are nice.	Dogs are **nicer** than cats.
Kittens are cute.	Kittens are **cuter** than puppies.

For 1 syllable adjectives that ends in vowel + consonant, double the consonant and add *-er.*

big → big**ger**	thin → thin**ner**
fat → fat**ter**	sad → sad**der**
Pigs are fat.	Pigs are **fatter** than donkeys.
Cows are big.	Cows are **bigger** than sheep.

For adjectives that end in *consonant + -y*, change the *-y* to *-i* and add *-er.*

easy → eas**ier**	dirty → dirt**ier**
pretty → prett**ier**	happy → happ**ier**
Their rooster looks pretty.	Their rooster looks **prettier** than ours.
Your horses look happy.	Your horses look **happier** than mine.

For adjectives with 2 or more syllables, except those ending in *-y*, use **more** + base adjective.

beautiful → **more** beautiful	common → **more** common
popular → **more** popular	careful → **more** careful
Feathers are beautiful.	Feathers are **more beautiful** than fur.
Dogs are popular.	Dogs are **more popular** pets than birds.

There are common adjectives that have irregular comparative forms.

bad → **worse**	little → **less**
good → **better**	much → **more**
far → **farther**	
Dogs are *good* pets.	Dogs are **better** pets than cats.
Roosters are *bad* pets.	Roosters are **worse** pets than cats.

Regular adjectives describe a specific noun. Comparative adjectives are used to compare nouns. Comparative adjectives show that one noun has **more** quality of an adjective than another noun.

For most adjectives, the comparative form adds *-er.* There are other spelling rules that depend on the ending of the adjective.

soft → **softer**
   add *-er*

nice → **nicer**
   remove silent *-e*, add *-er*

big → **bigger**
   double consonant, add *-er*

easy → **easier**
   change *-y* to *-i*, add *-er*

beautiful → **more** beautiful
   use **more** + base adjective

To compare two nouns, use a comparative adjective followed by the word *than*. This is known as a statement of superiority.

comparative adjective + than

Exercises

A: Write the **comparative** form of the adjective.

1. soft _softer_
2. nice _____
3. big _____
4. easy _____
5. beautiful _____
6. heavy _____
7. bad _____
8. sad _____
9. close _____
10. cute _____

11. easy _____
12. happy _____
13. good _____
14. far _____
15. popular _____
16. pretty _____
17. fat _____
18. short _____
19. dirty _____
20. thin _____

B: Make **comparative statements** of **superiority**. Follow the example.

1. **rooster** The chicken is fast.   _The rooster is **faster than** the chicken._

2. **cat** The dog is soft.   _____

3. **pig** The donkey is dirty.   _____

4. **Jane** Mary is beautiful.   _____

5. **Henry** Greg is tall.   _____

6. **kitten** The puppy is cute.   _____

7. **cow** The sheep is big.   _____

8. **hospital** The church is close.   _____

9. **division** Addition is easy.   _____

10. **Marty** Steve is nice.   _____

C: Make **comparative statements** of **superiority.** Use the given adjectives.

1. Henry's dog weighs 10 pounds. Alice's dog weighs 5 pounds. **(heavy)**

Henry's dog **is heavier than** Alice's dog.

2. Judy's horse is 7 years old. Amy's horse is 3 years old. **(old)**

3. Harry's pig is 4 feet tall. Jim's pig is 3 feet tall. **(tall)**

4. Mary's cat is 7 years old. John's cat is 10 year old. **(young)**

5. The horse's tail is 4 feet long. The donkey's tail is 2 feet long. **(long)**

6. Alan is five feet six inches. Teddy is six feet five inches. **(short)**

7. I walk 5 miles every day. You walk 4 miles every day. **(far)**

8. My dog sleeps all day. Your dog sleeps a little at night. **(lazy)**

9. The rooster's tail feathers are long. The chicken's tail feathers are short. **(long)**

10. The kittens are very popular with the children. The cats are less popular with the children.
(popular)

Exercises

D: Read the story and answer the questions. Follow the example.

Alice had a very fun weekend. On Saturday morning Alice visited the ABC pet store with her friend Stacey. Alice was shopping for a new collar for her dog Jack. It was loud inside the pet store. The puppies were barking. The birds were noisy. The puppies were noisier than the birds. Alice found the pet collars. The store had cat collars and dog collars. The dog collars were more expensive than the cat collars. Alice chose a large, red collar for Jack. Stacey bought food for her new kittens.

On Sunday Alice went with her brother Eric to their grandparent's farm. Her grandparents have chickens, pigs, cows and one horse. The horse's name is Trigger. Alice rode Trigger while Eric was feeding the chickens. Trigger was cleaner than the other farm animals. Alice's grandfather gives Trigger a bath every day. After her ride, Alice and Eric went home. It was a great weekend.

1. Where did Alice go on Saturday morning?

Alice went to the ABC pet store on Saturday morning.

2. Were the puppies noisier than the birds?

_____

3. Were the cat collars more expensive than the dog collars?

_____

4. Where did Alice go with her brother on Sunday?

_____

5. What did Alice do while Eric was feeding the chickens?

_____

6. Was Trigger dirtier than the other farm animals?

_____

Exercises

E: Follow the example.

1. loud / quiet

Roosters are loud.

Is a rooster louder than a chicken?

Yes, a rooster is louder than a chicken.

Chickens are quieter than roosters.

2. dirty / clean

3. big / small

4. soft / hard

5. fast / slow

Exercises

F: Listen to the story and choose the correct answer.
Visit **www.basicesl.com/workbook-2/lesson-25** to listen to the story.

1. Gloria lives ___*on a farm*___ .

                                                    a. in the city   **b.** in Spain   **(c.)** on a farm

2. There are _____ chickens on the farm.

                                                    a. two   **b.** three   **c.** four

3. The black horse is _____ than the brown horse.

                                                    a. bigger   **b.** longer   **c.** smaller

4. The cows are both _____ .

                                                    a. back   **b.** white   **c.** brown

5. The pig with the stripe is the _____ pig.

                                                    a. bigger   **b.** smaller   **c.** meaner

6. The rooster is _____ .

                                                    a. mean   **b.** popular   **c.** loud

7. There are a lot of _____ that live around the farm.

                                                    a. birds   **b.** cats   **c.** sheep

8. Gloria found a _____ on her walk.

                                                    a. feather   **b.** wing   **c.** beak

Workbook 2
Animals
Lesson 26: Wild Animals
Superlative adjectives

 basicesl.com/workbook-2/lesson-26

- ☐ Watch vocabulary video. Listen and repeat.
- ☐ Complete vocabulary exercises. (**Download**)
- ☐ Watch grammar video. Listen and repeat.
- ☐ Complete grammar exercises. (**Workbook**)
- ☐ Complete extra grammar exercises. (**Download**)
- ☐ Take a quiz. (**Download**)

Vocabulary

1. tiger	2. lion	3. elephant	4. giraffe
5. bear	6. wolf	7. gorilla	8. monkey
9. snake	10. frog	11. crocodile	12. turtle
13. owl	14. eagle	15. deer	16. rat
17. fang	18. claw	19. trunk	20. shell

21. all (*adj, pron*) **22.** fast (*adj*) **23.** slow (*adj*)

24. strong (*adj*) **25.** weak (*adj*) **26.** wild (*adj*)

27. dangerous (*adj*) **28.** deadly (*adj*) **29.** scary (*adj*)

Irregular verb list page 6

Grammar

Superlative adjectives

For most adjectives, add -*est*

wild → wild**est**	Which giraffe is the **tallest**?
fast → fast**est**	The first giraffe is *tall*.
slow → slow**est**	The second giraffe is *taller*.
tall → tall**est**	The third giraffe is the **tallest**.

For adjectives that end in a silent -*e*, remove the -*e* and add -*est*

nice → **nicest**	Which turtle is *close* to the food?
large → **largest**	The nice turtle is *close* to me.
cute → **cutest**	The mean turtle is *closer* to you.
close → **closest**	The old one is closest to the food.

For 1 syllable adjectives that end vowel + consonant, double the consonant and add -*est*.

sad → **saddest**	What animals are *big*?
fat → **fattest**	Wolves are *big*.
thin → **thinnest**	Lions are *bigger* than wolves.
big → **biggest**	Bears are the **biggest** of the three.

For adjectives that end in *consonant* + -*y*, remove the -*y*, add -*iest*

deadly → **deadliest**	How *scary* are the rats?
scary → **scariest**	Rats are very *scary*.
heavy → **heaviest**	Snakes are *scarier* than rats.
angry → **angriest**	Crocodiles are the **scariest**.

For adjectives with 3 or more syllables, use **most** + base adjective.

different → **most** different	What animals are *dangerous*?
delicious → **most** delicious	Eagles are *dangerous*.
terrible → **most** terrible	Monkeys are *more dangerous*.
dangerous → **most** dangerous	Tigers are the **most dangerous.**

There are common adjectives that have irregular superlative forms.

bad → **worst**	Which animals are *bad* pets?
good → **best**	Owls are *bad* pets.
far → **farthest**	Deer are *worse* pets than owls.
little → **least (amount)**	Gorillas are the **worst** pets of all.
much → **most**	

Regular adjectives describe nouns. Comparative adjectives compare two nouns. Superlative adjectives show which noun has the **most** quality of an adjective.

For most adjectives, the superlative form adds -*est*. There are other spelling rules that depend on the ending of the adjective.

wild → **wildest**
   add -*est*

nice → **nicest**
   remove silent -*e*, add -*est*

big → **biggest**
   double consonant, add -*est*

easy → **easiest**
   change -*y* to -*i*, add -*est*

beautiful → **most** beautiful
   use **most** + base adjective

Exercises

A: Write the **superlative** form of the adjective.

1. short _shortest_

2. close _____

3. thin _____

4. deadly _____

5. careful _____

6. bad _____

7. tall _____

8. cute _____

9. big _____

10. small _____

11. scary _____

12. large _____

13. fat _____

14. angry _____

15. good _____

16. much _____

17. wild _____

18. dirty _____

19. beautiful _____

20. far _____

B: Answer the questions with an **adjective**, a **comparative adjective**, and a **superlative adjective**.

1. fast

Wolves are _fast_ .

Tigers are _faster_ than wolves.

Lions are the _fastest_ .

2. scary

Rats are _____ .

Snakes are _____ than rats.

Crocodiles are the _____ .

3. strong

Monkeys are _____ .

Gorillas are _____ than monkeys.

Bears are the _____ .

4. quick

Pigs are _____ .

Dogs are _____ than pigs.

Cats are the _____ .

5. beautiful

Snakes are _____ .

Deer are _____ than snakes.

Owls are the _____ .

6. cute

Turtles are _____ .

Puppies are _____ than turtles.

Kittens are the _____ .

Exercises

C: Write two sentences with **superlative** adjectives. Use the given clues. Follow the example.

1. The brown bear is 10 years old. The black bear is 9 years old. The white bear is 15 years old.

(old / young)   *The white bear is the oldest. The black bear is the youngest.*

2. The giraffe is 18 feet tall. The elephant is 13 feet tall. The horse is 6 ft tall.

(tall / short) _____

3. The tiger weighs 200 pounds. The wolf weighs 100 pounds. The dog weighs 15 pounds.

(heavy / light) _____

4. The donkey's tail is 2 feet long. The horse's tail is 3 feet long. The elephant's tail is 4 feet long.

(long / short) _____

5. The cat has 30 teeth. The dog has 42 teeth. The crocodile has 64 teeth.

(much / little) _____

6. The dog carried 25 pounds. The horse carried 150 pounds. The elephant carried 300 pounds.

(strong / weak) _____

7. Elephants run 15 miles per hour. Bears run 35 miles per hour. Turtles run 3 miles per hour.

(fast / slow) _____

8. Andy's house is 3 miles away. Erin's house is 1 mile way. Rudy's house is 15 miles away.

(far / close) _____

9. I was born in March of 2002. Dan was born in May of 2002. Ellen was born in July of 2002.

(old / young) _____

10. The white shell is very nice. The brown shell is okay. The red shell is not good.

(good / bad) _____

Exercises

1. deadly / animal

*How **deadly** are these animals?*

*Snakes are **deadly** animals.*

*Crocodiles are **deadlier** than snakes.*

*Lions are the **deadliest** of all these animals.*

2. quick / bird

3. smart / pet

4. dirty / animal

5. expensive / tools

Exercises

E: Read the story and answer the questions. Use complete sentences.

My name is David. Last year my parents, my brother Andy, and I took a camping trip to Mount Rainier. It was the best trip of my life. We saw many wild animals. On the very first day of the trip we saw three deer, one bear, and a gray wolf. The wolf was the most beautiful animal we saw on our first day.

On the second day of our trip we saw many wild birds. Andy saw an eagle high in the sky. After sunset, my mother saw an owl sitting on a tree branch near the river. The trees near the river were the biggest ones in the park. Andy told me the most dangerous animals in the park were the lions and the tigers. I knew there weren't any lions or tigers. I told him the worst animals in the park were bears and snakes.

On the third day of our trip we took a long walk up the mountain. We saw three more bears less than 30 feet away. It was the scariest day of my life.

1. How good was David's <u>trip</u> to Mount Rainier?

It was the best trip of his life.

2. How beautiful was the gray wolf?

_____

3. Where did David's mother see the owl?

_____

4. How big were the trees near the river?

_____

5. What did David tell Andy about bears and snakes?

_____

6. Why was the third day the scariest day of David's life?

_____

_____

Exercises

1. Andrea has a dog, a cat and a small ___*turtle*___ .

        a. wolf   **b.** frog   **c.** turtle

2. Andrea's dog is the _____ of her pets.

        a. biggest   **b.** slowest   **c.** wildest

3. Andrea's turtle is smaller than the _____ .

        a. dog   **b.** cat   **c.** a & b

4. Andrea's dog used to look like a _____ .

        a. cat   **b.** wolf   **c.** tiger

5. Andrea saw a wolf at the _____ .

        a. river   **b.** lake   **c.** National Park

6. Andrea thinks bears are _____ .

        a. scary   **b.** dangerous   **c.** smart

7. _____ are one of the fastest animals.

        a. tigers   **b.** giraffes   **c.** lions

8. Giraffes are the _____ animals.

        a. shortest   **b.** tallest   **c.** fattest

Workbook 2
Animals
Lesson 27: Ocean Animals & Insects

Expressing inequality

Expressing equality

 basicesl.com/workbook-2/lesson-27

☐ Watch vocabulary video. Listen and repeat.

☐ Complete vocabulary exercises. (**Download**)

☐ Watch grammar video. Listen and repeat.

☐ Complete grammar exercises. (**Workbook**)

☐ Complete extra grammar exercises. (**Download**)

☐ Take a quiz. (**Download**)

Vocabulary

1. octopus	**2.** whale	**3.** shark	**4.** dolphin
5. jellyfish	**6.** crab	**7.** seal	**8.** penguin
9. bee	**10.** fly	**11.** butterfly	**12.** mosquito
13. ant	**14.** spider	**15.** flea	**16.** cricket
17. web	**18.** hive	**19.** coral	**20.** nest

21. violent (*adj*)   **22.** gentle (*adj*)   **23.** gross (*adj*)

24. smooth (*adj*)   **25.** rough (*adj*)   **26.** noisy (*adj*)

27. friendly (*adj*)   **28.** to swim (*verb*)   **29.** to fly (*verb*)

* Irregular verb list page 6

Grammar

Statements of equality and inequality

Statement	Statement of equality
Dolphins are friendly.	Dolphins are **as friendly as** dogs.
Blue whales live a long time.	Blue whales live **as long as** elephants.
Butterflies are gentle.	Butterflies are **as gentle as** turtles.
Some octopuses are very big.	Some octopuses are **as big as** a car.
Bee wings are thin.	Bee wings are **as thin as** paper.

Statement	Statement of inequality
Bees are small.	Crickets are not **as small as** bees.
Sharks swim fast.	Seals do not swim **as fast as** sharks.
Crabs are slow.	Penguins are not **as slow as** crabs.
Fleas are gross.	Mosquitoes are not **as gross as** fleas.
Corals look smooth.	Hives don't look **as smooth as** corals.

Statement of inequality	Comparative statement
Ants aren't **as noisy as** bees.	Bees are **noisier** than ants.
Penguins aren't **as fast as** sharks.	Sharks are **faster** than penguins.
Dolphins aren't **as loud as** seals.	Seals are **louder** than dolphins.
Fleas aren't **as big as** spiders.	Spiders are **bigger** than fleas.

Question	Answer
Are bees **as scary as** spiders?	Yes, bees are **as scary as** spiders. No, bees aren't **as scary as** spiders.
Do whales eat **as much as** sharks?	Yes, whales eat **as much as** sharks. No, whales don't eat **as much as** sharks.
Is a web **as strong as** a nest?	Yes, a web is **as strong as** a nest. No, a web isn't **as strong as** a nest.
Which is **noisier**, an ant or a bee?	A bee is **noisier** than an ant. An ant isn't **as noisy as** a bee.
Which flies **faster**, a mosquito or a fly?	A fly flies **faster** than a mosquito. A mosquito doesn't fly **as fast as** a fly.
Which is **friendlier**, a seal or a dolphin?	A dolphin is **friendlier** than a seal. A seal isn't **as friendly as** a dolphin.

Statements of equality show that one noun has the **same** quality of the adjective as another noun.

as + **adjective** + **as**

Statements of inequality show that one noun has **less** quality of the adjective than another noun.

not + **as** + **adjective** + **as**

Exercises

1. to swim _swam_

2. to make _____

3. to fly _____

4. to give _____

5. to understand _____

6. to drink _____

7. to find _____

8. to keep _____

9. to lose _____

10. to leave _____

11. to come _____

12. to hit _____

13. to build _____

14. to bring _____

15. to bend _____

16. to tell _____

17. to eat _____

18. to get _____

19. to tear _____

20. to break _____

B: Use the clues to write a statement of **inequality**. Follow the example.

1. small _Butterflies **are not as small as** mosquitoes._

2. noisy _____

3. gentle _____

4. beautiful _____

5. big _____

6. gross _____

7. fast _____

8. silent _____

C: Change the comparative statement to a statement of **inequality**.

1. The shark is more dangerous than the whale.

*The whale **is not as dangerous as** the shark.*

2. Dolphins are friendlier than sharks.

_____

3. The sea coral is more beautiful than the spider web.

_____

4. Harry's puppy is cuter than Molly's puppy.

_____

5. The horse is faster than the donkey.

_____

6. My dogs are gentler than your dogs.

_____

7. The pink pigs are dirtier than the black pigs.

_____

8. The bee hive is bigger than the spider web.

_____

9. Octopuses are quicker than jellyfish.

_____

10. The electric drill is more expensive than the hammer.

_____

Exercises

D: Read the story and answer the questions in complete sentences. Follow the example.

The ocean is full of animals. Popular ocean animals are animals like whales, sharks and dolphins. Dolphins and whales are very smart. Dolphins are not as aggressive as whales and sharks. A dolphin is not as large as a shark. Sharks are not as large as whales.

Other popular ocean animals are seals and penguins. Penguins and seals live in the ocean and on land. Seals swim after penguins in the water. Penguins are not as fast as seals.

Deep in the ocean are animals like octopus, jellyfish and crab. Octopus eat jellyfish and crabs. Ocean turtles also eat jellyfish and some corals.

Turtles put their eggs in nests. Some penguins don't make nests. They stand above their eggs. The father penguin looks after the egg while the mother finds food in the ocean.

1. Are dolphins as aggressive as whales and sharks?

No, dolphins are not as aggressive as whales and sharks.

2. Are sharks as large as whales?

_____

3. Where do penguins and seals live?

_____

4. Are seals faster than penguins?

_____

5. What do octopus eat?

_____

6. Do turtles put their eggs in nests?

_____

E: Follow the example.

1. mean / a lot

*Are whales **as mean as** sharks?*

*No, whales **are not as mean as** sharks.*

*Sharks **are <u>a lot</u> meaner than** whales.*

2. fast / a little

3. noisy / much

4. deadly / a lot

5. scary / much

Exercises

F: Listen to the story and choose the correct answer.
Visit **www.basicesl.com/workbook-2/lesson-27** to listen to the story.

1. Barry studies insects at __*school*__ .

        a. home   **b.** the library   **c.** school

2. Barry likes bees and _____ .

        a. crickets   **b.** mosquitoes   **c.** ants

3. Bees are _____ many common spiders.

        a. as dangerous as   **b.** not as dangerous as

4. Barry is _____ when he sees a bees nest.

        a. careful   **b.** gentle   **c.** smooth

5. Barry looks for _____ after school.

        a. bee hives   **b.** spider webs   **c.** fleas

6. The spider webs at Barry's house are _____ than the spider webs at his school.

        a. smaller   **b.** bigger   **c.** grosser

7. The bee hive was _____ the yard.

        a. around   **b.** in   **c.** on

8. Barry's father was _____ when he removed the bee hive from the house.

.   **a.** gentle   **b.** violent   **c.** friendly

Workbook 2
Sports
Lesson 28: Sports
Adverbs of manner

 basicesl.com/workbook-2/lesson-28

☐   Watch vocabulary video. Listen and repeat.

☐   Complete vocabulary exercises. (**Download**)

☐   Watch grammar video. Listen and repeat.

☐   Complete grammar exercises. (**Workbook**)

☐   Complete extra grammar exercises. (**Download**)

☐   Take a quiz. (**Download**)

Vocabulary

1. soccer	**2.** football	**3.** basketball	**4.** baseball
5. field	**6.** stadium	**7.** court	**8.** game
9. team	**10.** player	**11.** fan	**12.** referee
13. teammate	**14.** goal	**15.** score	**16.** point
17. to throw (*verb**)	**18.** to catch (*verb**)	**19.** to pitch (*verb*)	**20.** to swing (*verb**)

21. crazy (*adj*)	**22.** careless (*adj*)	**23.** simple (*adj*)
24. to watch (*verb*)	**25.** to cheer (*verb*)	**26.** to follow (*verb*)
27. to win (*verb**)	**28.** to lose (*verb**)	**29.** to score (*verb*)

* Irregular verb list page 6

Adverbs of manner

For most adjectives, add -**ly**.

quick → quick**ly**	loud → loud**ly**
polite → polite**ly**	rude → rude**ly**
That player was *quick*.	That player moved **quickly**.
The fans were *loud*.	The fans cheered **loudly**.

For adjectives ending in -*y*, change -*y* to -*i* and add -**ly**.

angry → angr**ily**	lazy → laz**ily**
easy → eas**ily**	noisy → nois**ily**
The coach was *angry*.	She yelled at the team **angrily**.
The teammate was *lazy*.	He walked down the court **lazily**.

For adjectives ending in *consonant* + -*le*, remove -*le,* and add -**ly**.

terrible → terrib**ly**	gentle → gent**ly**
simple → simp**ly**	comfortable → comfortab**ly**
Those referees were *terrible*.	They were **terribly** rude to us.
Dave is *gentle* with the children.	He is **gently** kicking the ball to them.

For some adverbs, there are no spelling rules.

good → **well**	hard → **hard**
fast → **fast**	straight → **straight**
Will is a *good* baseball player.	He pitched **well** today.
Football is a *hard* game.	The teams try very **hard**.

The question word *how* is used to ask about the manner in which something happens. Adverbs of manner help us describe the manner.

Question	Answer
How did I throw the baseball?	You threw the baseball **fast**.
How did our team play today?	Our team played **well**.
How does Pam throw the football?	She throws the football **hard**.
How do fans talk to the referees?	The fans talk to them **rudely**.

Adverbs are used to express how something happens or how something is done. Adverbs describe verbs, adjectives and other adverbs.

Most adverbs of manner are formed by adding -*ly* to adjectives. There are other spelling rules that depend on the ending of the adjective.

    most adjectives → add -**ly**
    ends in -*y* → change -*y* to -*i*,
        and add -**ly**
    ends in *consonant* + -*le* →
        remove -*le* and add -**ly**

There are some irregular adverbs of manner that do not follow spelling rules.

Adverbs of manner are usually placed after the main verb or at the end of the sentence. They may also appear before the main verb.

Exercises

A: Form adverbs of manner from the given adjective.

1. slow _slowly_

2. careless _____

3. bad _____

4. careful _____

5. different _____

6. crazy _____

7. loose _____

8. loud _____

9. hard _____

10. honest _____

11. beautiful _____

12. sad _____

13. nice _____

14. mean _____

15. shy _____

16. kind _____

17. good _____

18. rude _____

19. fast _____

20. lazy _____

21. weak _____

22. tight _____

23. terrible _____

24. simple _____

25. light _____

26. calm _____

27. angry _____

28. correct _____

29. soft _____

30. heavy _____

B: Is the **bold** word an adjective **(adj)** or adverb **(adv)**?

1. _adj_ Their players are **strong**.

2. _____ The **rude** fan left the stadium.

3. _____ The team played **well**.

4. _____ The referee spoke **loudly**.

5. _____ The field was **beautiful**.

6. _____ The **better** team won the game.

7. _____ The player threw the baseball **fast**.

8. _____ Coach watched his team **carefully**.

9. _____ Baseballs are **hard**.

10. _____ Donald threw the baseball **hard**.

Exercises

C: Use the given word as an adjective and adverb to complete the sentences. Follow the example

1. (good) Joe and Ray are __good__ players. They played __well__ today.

2. (bad) We had a _____ game. We played _____ yesterday.

3. (simple) Baseball is a _____ game. You _____ hit the ball.

4. (loud) The fans cheered _____. Robert and Sheila are _____ .

5. (fast) The _____ player scored. The teammates ran _____ .

6. (loose) Greg doesn't wear his pants _____ . His belt isn't _____ .

7. (kind) Mike is _____ . Mike speaks _____ of Mary.

8. (happy) Jane is _____ for the team. She cheered _____ .

9. (hard) Jake hit the ball _____ . The baseball is _____ .

10. (serious) Be _____ this time please. Take the game _____ .

D: Correct the **past** tense sentence. Use a correct <u>adverb</u>.

1. The team runned on the field <u>quick</u>. The *team* **ran** *on* the *field* **quickly**.

2. The boy throwed the ball fastly. _____

3. The fans leaved the stadium slow. _____

4. The team losed the game bad. _____

5. The referee speaked loud to the coach. _____

6. The children play quiet. _____

7. John drived careful to the game. _____

8. The girls putted the ball away careless. _____

9. The principal quick readed the scores. _____

10. The coach kind taked us to the game. _____

Exercises

John played basketball in high school. John was taller than most of his teammates. He was the second best player on the team. John's coach Gina made her players play hard. In most games, John's teammates played well. In some games, John and his teammates played carelessly. John's team lost their last game because they weren't careful.

John's team was winning by one point in the last thirty seconds of the game. John lazily threw the ball to his teammate Chris. Chris didn't catch the ball. The other team caught the ball and scored. John's team lost by one point. All the players on his team stood sadly on the court.

There were a lot of fans at John's game. Some fans cheered loudly for the other team because they won. John's parents watched quietly. John's team politely left the court. After the game the fans and the other team talked and laughed happily.

1. How good was <u>John</u> at playing basketball?

<u>He</u> was the second best player on the team.

2. How did the coach make the players play?

_____

3. Why did John's team lose their last game?

_____

4. How did John throw the ball?

_____

5. What did John's team do after the other team caught the ball and scored?

_____

6. What did John's team do after the game?

_____

F: Follow the example.

1. aggressive / <u>to play</u> (on)

| | John / Jake |

*Is John **aggressive** on the field?*

*No, **he's not** aggressive on the field.*

*Jake is **more aggressive** than him.*

*Jake <u>plays</u> **aggressively** on the field.*

2. fast / to run (on)

| | Alison / Andrea |

3. loud / to talk (at)

| | the referees / the players |

4. wild / to cheer (in)

| | you / my uncle |

5. quiet / to read

| | I / your brother |

Exercises

G: Listen to the story. Choose the correct answer.
Visit **www.basicesl.com/workbook-2/lesson-28** to listen to the story.

1. Ruby plays _____three_____ sports at her school.

| | **a.** two | **b.** three | **c.** four |

2. Ruby's team is the _____ .

| | **a.** Lions | **b.** Bears | **c.** Eagles |

3. Ruby is one of the _____ players on her team.

| | **a.** worst | **b.** best | **c.** fastest |

4. Ruby tries hard and plays _____ most games.

| | **a.** good | **b.** better | **c.** well |

5. Ruby _____ two goals in her last game.

| | **a.** hit | **b.** scored | **c.** threw |

6. Ruby's family watched the game _____ .

| | **a.** calmly | **b.** closely | **c.** crazily |

7. Ruby's family cheered _____ .

| | **a.** crazily | **b.** loudly | **c.** rudely |

8. Ruby's family hugged her _____ .

| | **a.** carelessly | **b.** loosely | **c.** tightly |

Workbook 2
Sports
Lesson 29: Equipment
Adverbs of time
Adverbs of frequency

 basicesl.com/workbook-2/lesson-29

☐	Watch vocabulary video. Listen and repeat.
☐	Complete vocabulary exercises. (**Download**)
☐	Watch grammar video. Listen and repeat.
☐	Complete grammar exercises. (**Workbook**)
☐	Complete extra grammar exercises. (**Download**)
☐	Take a quiz. (**Download**)

Vocabulary

1. ball	**2.** bat	**3.** pads	**4.** cleats
5. uniform	**6.** helmet	**7.** volleyball	**8.** net
9. tennis	**10.** racket	**11.** golf	**12.** club
13. to ski	**14.** skis	**15.** to surf	**16.** surfboard
17. to dribble	**18.** to shoot	**19.** to guard	**20.** to block

21. equipment (*noun*)   **22.** only (*adv*)   **23.** too (*adv*)

24. to fall (*verb**)   **25.** to yell (*verb*)   **26.** to hold (*verb**)

27. to own (*verb*)   **28.** to belong (*verb*)   **29.** to steal (*verb**)

* Irregular verb list page 6

Adverbs of time

Definite: *now, then, yesterday, today, tonight, tomorrow*

Jordan skied **yesterday**.
Kelly surfed with me **today**.
Natalie swims **tomorrow**.

Miguel is shooting the ball **now**.
Wash your uniform **tonight**.
David belonged to our team **then**.

Indefinite: *later, late, early, soon, eventually, recently, yet, already*

We are exercising **soon**.
The team got there **early**.
Our coach left here **late**.
Let's play golf **later**.

We played volleyball **recently**.
They lost the game **eventually**.
Our team stole the ball **already**.
He didn't put on his helmet **yet**.

Question	Answer
When did he buy that bat?	He bought that bat **yesterday**.
When does the game begin?	The game begins **now**.
When do we meet the players?	We meet the players **later**.
When do we get our new cleats?	You get your new cleats **soon**.

Adverbs of time show **when** the action of the verb takes place.

Definite time adverbs express specific points in time.

Indefinite time adverbs express a time relative to another time. Indefinite times are not specific.

Time adverbs are usually placed at the end of the sentence.

Adverbs of frequency

Definite: *once, twice, hourly, daily, weekly, monthly*

She surfed this beach **once**.
Paul hit the net **twice**.
More fans are arriving **hourly**.

Our team exercises **daily**.
Diego plays soccer **weekly**.
I break a tennis racket **monthly**.

Indefinite: *always, never, usually, rarely, often, frequently, constantly*

They **always** surf in Malibu.
She **never** skis in Aspen.
We **rarely** stretch before games.
You **often** hold the club too tight.

I am **usually** in my uniform.
We are **frequently** at the stadium.
Coach is **constantly** yelling at us.

Question	Answer
How often did Bill block you?	He only blocked me **once**.
How often did you guard Sue?	I guarded her at games **weekly**.
How often did I fall off the surfboard?	You **rarely** fell off of it.
How often did Debra dribble the ball?	She **never** dribbled the ball.

Adverbs of frequency show **how often** the verb takes place.

Definite frequency adverbs express an exact frequency. They are usually placed at the end of a statement.

Indefinite frequency adverbs express an approximate frequency. They are usually placed before the main verb, or after the verb *to be*.

Questions about frequency generally begin with the question word *how* plus the adverb *often*.

Exercises

A: Write the simple past tense of the verb.

1. to go   _went_

2. to wear _____

3. to run _____

4. to hold _____

5. to stand _____

6. to win _____

7. to tear _____

8. to shoot _____

9. to catch _____

10. to fit _____

11. to block _____

12. to sit _____

13. to guard _____

14. to buy _____

15. to dribble _____

16. to know _____

17. to surf _____

18. to write _____

19. to ski _____

20. to break _____

B: Complete the sentence using the given adverb of time.

1. today John is surfing.   _John is surfing **today**._

2. soon My new cleats and bats arrive.   _____

3. later We are golfing.   _____

4. tomorrow Yes, John plays tennis.   _____

5. now Jerry is guarding the goal.   _____

6. tonight We are surfing.   _____

7. later They are coming.   _____

8. early Eric surfs at the beach.   _____

9. then I was playing volleyball.   _____

10. yesterday Lindsey skied down the hill.   _____

C: Complete the sentence using adverbs frequency.

1. always John surfs with his friends.
John **always** surfs with his friends

2. rarely John surfs in the morning.
_____

3. twice I hit the ball hard.
_____

4. never Derrick shoots the ball.
_____

5. frequently Ann forgets her cleats.
_____

6. weekly I break a racket.
_____

7. hourly Volleyball games begin.
_____

8. usually I ski at night.
_____

9. monthly Dan and Sharon golf.
_____

10. once I yelled during the game.
_____

D: Rewrite the sentences and include the given adverb in both sentences.

1. usually The uniforms <u>are</u> clean. We <u>wash</u> them before the games.

The uniforms <u>are</u> **usually** clean. We **usually** <u>wash</u> them before the games

2. often The bats are heavy. David swings them before the games.

_____

3. always The helmets are dirty. They drop their helmets on the field.

_____

4. daily The girls were at the park. They ran around the park.

_____

5. constantly Terry is surfing. He surfed.

_____

6. rarely The uniforms are white. The players wear white uniforms.

Exercises

E: Follow the example. Write two sentences. For the second sentence choose the best indefinite frequency adverb: **always**, **frequently**, **never**, **often**, and **rarely**.

this week	Sunday	Monday	Tuesday	Wednesday	Thursday	Friday	Saturday
1. Sarah to play golf				⛳			
2. Billy to shoot basketball	🏀		🏀		🏀		
3. Jackie to steal soccer ball	⚽	⚽	⚽	⚽	⚽	⚽	⚽
4. family to lose skis							
5. Tim and I to go stadium	🏟	🏟	🏟	🏟		🏟	🏟

1. _Sarah played golf **one time** this week._

    She **rarely** plays golf.

2. _____

    _____

3. _____

    _____

4. _____

    _____

5. _____

    _____

F: Follow the example. Use the given clues.

1. John / to get / yesterday

to wear / rarely

When did John get his helmet?

He got it **yesterday**.

How often does he wear his helmet?

He **rarely** wears it.

2. Ashley / to buy / recently

to use / frequently

3. Henry / to fix / today

to clean / daily

4. players / to choose / yesterday

to wear / weekly

5. girls / to use / tonight

to break / never

Exercises

1. Tom plays soccer, basketball and <u> *baseball* </u> .

                                        a. baseball   **b.** tennis   **c.** volleyball

2. Tom always wears a _____ for the soccer games.

                                        a. red uniform **b.** white pads **c.** blue hat

3. The basketball team practices _____ .

                                        a. daily   **b.** monthly   **c.** weekly

4. Tom dribbles _____ he shoots.

                                        a. more than **b.** less than **c.** as much as

5. Tom's coach is _____ happy.

                                        a. always   **b.** often   **c.** never

6. Tom's baseball uniforms are white and _____ .

                                        a. blue   **b.** red   **c.** green

7. The bats and helmets belong to _____ .

                                        a. Tom   **b.** coach   **c.** the school

8. Tom's hits the ball out of the park _____ .

                                        a. always   **b.** often   **c.** daily

Workbook 2

Sports

Lesson 30: Athlete

Indefinite people, places, and things

 basicesl.com/workbook-2/lesson-30

☐ Watch vocabulary video. Listen and repeat.

☐ Complete vocabulary exercises. (**Download**)

☐ Watch grammar video. Listen and repeat.

☐ Complete grammar exercises. (**Workbook**)

☐ Complete extra grammar exercises. (**Download**)

☐ Take a quiz. (**Download**)

Vocabulary

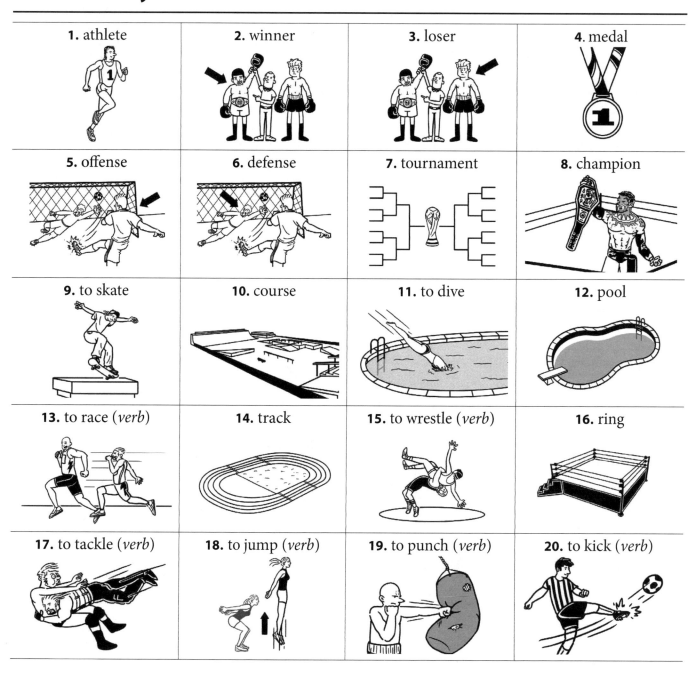

1. athlete	**2.** winner	**3.** loser	**4.** medal
5. offense	**6.** defense	**7.** tournament	**8.** champion
9. to skate	**10.** course	**11.** to dive	**12.** pool
13. to race (*verb*)	**14.** track	**15.** to wrestle (*verb*)	**16.** ring
17. to tackle (*verb*)	**18.** to jump (*verb*)	**19.** to punch (*verb*)	**20.** to kick (*verb*)

21. all (*adj*)

22. none (*adj*)

23. match (*noun*)

24. to practice (*verb*)

25. to exercise (*verb*)

26. to stretch (*verb*)

27. to fight (*verb**)

28. to beat (*verb**)

29. to lead (*verb**)

* Irregular verb list page 6

Grammar

Indefinite people, places, and things

	People (body / one)	**Places** (where)	**Things**
every-	everybody / everyone	everywhere	everything
no-	nobody / no-one	nowhere	nothing
some-	somebody / someone	somewhere	something
any-	anybody / anyone	anywhere	anything

Indefinite	**Specific**
Everyone is a winner.	*All of the athletes* are winners.
Nobody won the tournament.	*The team* didn't win the tournament.
Somebody kicked the ball twice.	*Alex and I* kicked the ball twice.
Sally didn't cheer for **anyone**.	Sally didn't cheer for *the champion*.
John swims **everywhere**.	John swims at *all the pools*.
We have **nowhere** to practice.	We have no *gym* to practice in.
Billy skated **somewhere**.	Billy skated to *the park*.
Pam wasn't racing **anywhere**.	Pam wasn't racing *at the tracks*.
Sarah plays **everything**.	Sarah plays *offense and defense*.
Jake does **nothing** before games.	Jake doesn't *exercise* before games.
Did Ally win **something**?	Did Ally win *a medal*?
Did you watch **anything** today?	Did you watch *the match* today?

Question	**Answer**
Who stretches after the game?	**Everyone** stretches after the game.
	Nobody stretches after the game.
Did **anyone** tackle you?	Yes, **someone** tackled me.
	No, **no-one** tackled me.
Did James fight in the ring?	Yes, he fought in the ring yesterday.
	No, he didn't fight **anywhere**.
Did I win **something?**	Yes, you won a medal.
	No, you didn't win **anything**.

Indefinite words do not refer to a specific person, place or thing. Indefinite words are used when the speaker doesn't know or doesn't identify a specific person, place or thing.

Indefinite words that begin with *every-* refer to all people, places or things.

> **everyone** = all persons

Indefinite words beginning with *no-* refer to no persons, places or things.

> **nobody** = 0 persons

In statements and questions, indefinite words beginning with *some-* refer to 1 or more persons, places or things.

> **something** = 1+ things

In negative statements and questions indefinite words beginning with *any-* refer to 1 or more persons, places or things.

> **anywhere** = 1+ places

If the subject is an indefinite person or thing, use 3rd person singular verb forms.

> **Everybody** wins...
> **Somebody** is...

Exercises

A: Write the **past tense** of the given regular and irregular verbs.

1. meet _met_

2. sell _____

3. drive _____

4. shoot _____

5. dive _____

6. fit _____

7. fight _____

8. fall _____

9. lead _____

10. buy _____

11. begin _____

12. ride _____

13. forget _____

14. jump _____

15. beat _____

16. tackle _____

17. wear _____

18. punch _____

19. hold _____

20. kick _____

B: Complete the sentences with indefinite words. Use the word in bold to help choose the correct indefinite word. Follow the example.

1. **trophy** Did John win _something/anything_ ? No, he didn't win _anything_ .

2. **Phoenix** Did Sheila drive _____ ? Yes, she drove _____ .

3. **Pete** Did Tony fight _____ ? No, he didn't fight _____ .

4. **bats** Does John sell _____ ? Yes, he sells _____ .

5. **Florida** Did the boys go _____ ? Yes, he went _____ .

6. **Seth** Did the player tackle _____ ? No, he didn't tackle _____ .

7. **ball** Did Amanda throw _____ ? No, she didn't throw _____ .

8. **the park** Is Alex skating _____ ? No, he isn't skating _____ .

9. **Stephanie** Did you forget _____ ? No, he didn't forget _____ .

10. **uniform** Did you wear _____ ? Yes, I wore _____ .

Exercises

C: Complete the sentence with an **indefinite** word that begins with *every-* or *no-*.

1. What did John win? **(0 medals)** He won _____*nothing*_____.

2. What did he say about the champion? **(0 statements)** He said _____.

3. Who stretched before the game? **(0 people)** _____ stretched.

4. Where did the athletes run in the park? **(all places)** They ran _____ in the park.

5. Is all the food gone? **(all food)** Yes, the athletes ate _____.

6. Where can we skate? **(0 places)** I'm sorry, there is _____ to skate here.

7. Who raced today? **(all athletes)** _____ raced today.

8. Where are the tournaments held? **(all places)** The tournaments are held _____.

9. Did anyone dive into the pool? **(0 people)** _____ dove into the pool.

10. Did you bring the uniforms, pads, and cleats? **(all things)** Yes, I brought _____.

D: Answer the question. Use an **indefinite** word. Follow the example.

1. Did you find something? _No, I didn't find anything._

2. Do you see anyone? _Yes,_

3. Are you going somewhere? _No,_

4. Did you beat anyone? _Yes,_

5. Did he fight anyone? _No,_

6. Did you look everywhere? _Yes,_

7. Did he jump on someone? _No,_

8. Did you forget something? _Yes,_

9. Did you race anywhere in the city? _No,_

10. Did you begin anything? _Yes,_

Exercises

E: Read the dialog and answer the questions.

Jenny: Last weekend we went to a wrestling tournament at my brother's high school. My brother was in five matches. He easily won four of them. He got a silver medal.

Lucy: There is something scary and dangerous about wrestling. Does anybody ever get hurt?

Jenny: All of the athletes are very careful. Sometimes someone gets hurt, but usually nobody does. The rules do not let them punch or kick. What did you do last weekend Lucy?

Lucy: Last weekend I went with my cousin Sal and some of his friends to a skate park somewhere in Los Angeles. I don't remember the name of the park.

Jenny: That is something I've always wanted to do. Was it fun?

Lucy: It was a lot of fun. Everybody had a great time. I learned some new jumps and raced around the course for hours. Come with us next time.

1. What did <u>Jenny</u> do last weekend?

She went to a wrestling tournament at her brother's high school.

2. How many matches did Jenny's brother win? What did he win?

_____

_____

3. Do the rules let athletes punch and kick?

_____

4. Where did Lucy go last weekend?

_____

5. What did Lucy learn at the skate park?

_____

Exercises

F: Follow the example. Answer the first question with **yes** and the second question with **no**.

1. person (-*one*)
every-, every-, any-, no-

to wrestle   to win

*Did **everyone** wrestle at the tournament?*

*Yes, **everyone** wrestled at the tournament.*

*Did **anyone** win a medal?*

*No, **no-one** won a medal.*

2. thing
any-, some-, any-, no-

to help   to help

3. person (-*body*)
any-, every-, any-, no-

to meet   to practice

4. person (-*one*)
any-, every-, any-, no-

to beat   to punch

5. person (-*body*)
every-, every-, any-, no-

to cheer   to stop

Exercises

G: Listen to the story and choose the correct answer.
Visit **www.basicesl.com/workbook-2/lesson-30** to listen to the story.

1. Jen's soccer team practices __*daily*_____ .

       a. hourly   **b.** daily   **c.** weekly

2. First _____ stretches for ten minutes.

       a. everybody   **b.** somebody   **c.** nobody

3. The team runs around the _____ four times.

       a. pool   **b.** course   **c.** track

4. At practice the teams works on _____ .

       a. offense   **b.** defense   **c.** both

5. _____ always guards the goal.

       a. Jen   **b.** Coach   **c.** Someone

6. A soccer _____ is in San Diego.

       a. match   **b.** tournament   **c.** game

7. Who told Jen the winners get medals?

       a. everybody   **b.** somebody   **c.** The team

8. Jen's team usually plays the _____ .

       a. champions   **b.** losers   **c.** athletes

Workbook 2 • Lessons 16-30
www.basicesl.com/workbook-2

Answer Key

Lesson 16

Exercise A

1. You have **some** potatoes.

Do you have **any** tomatoes?

No, I don't have **any**.

2. You don't need **any** mushrooms.

Do you need **any** cucumbers?

Yes, I need **some** cucumbers.

3. Does the store have **any** broccoli?

No, it doesn't have **any** broccoli.

It doesn't have **any** lettuce .

4. Do you want **some** corn?

Yes, I want **some** corn.

I don't want **any** fruit.

5. Do you have **any** vegetables?

No, I don't have **any** vegetables.

Do you **want** some vegetables?

6. Do we need **any** onions?

No, we don't have **any**.

Do you want **some** onions?

Exercise B

1. Are there apples?

2. Is there lettuce?

3. Are there potatoes in the cupboard?

4. Are there green apples?

5. Are there any grapes for Jill?

6. Is there lemon in the water?

7. Is there a banana in the kitchen?

8. Are there strawberries in this drink?

9. Is there any onion in the food?

10. Is there any fruit on the table?

Exercise C

1. There are no vegetables.

There are not any vegetables.

2. There are no apples and oranges.

There are not any apples and oranges.

3. There is no juicy watermelon.

There is not any juicy watermelon.

4. There is no lemon in the cup.

There is not any lemon in the cup.

5. There are no sweet cherries in the bowl.

There are not any sweet cherries in the bowl.

Exercise D

1. Yes, you like some of the peppers.

No, you don't like any of the peppers.

2. Yes, it prepares some potatoes.

No, it doesn't prepare any potatoes.

3. Yes, it offers some coconuts today.

No, it doesn't offer any coconuts today.

4. Yes, they get some oranges.

No, they don't get any oranges.

5. Yes, she has some sweet potatoes.

No, she doesn't have any sweet potatoes.

6. Yes, we want some of your grapes.

No, we don't want any of your grapes.

Exercise E

1. Are there any apples in the kitchen?

No, there aren't any apples in the kitchen.

Are there any bananas?

Yes, there are some bananas.

2. Are there any potatoes on the plate?

No, there aren't any potatoes on the plate.

Is there any corn?

Yes, there is some corn.

3. Is there any pepper in the pan?

No, there isn't any pepper in the pan.

Is there any onion?

Yes, there is some onion.

4. Are there any cherries in the refrigerator?

No, there aren't any cherries in the refrigerator.

Are there any grapes?

Yes, there are some grapes.

5. Is there any watermelon in the bowl?

No, there isn't any watermelon in the bowl.

Is there any pineapple?

Yes, there is some pineapple.

Exercise F

1. Do they eat any carrots?

Henry eat some carrots.

Mary doesn't eat any carrots.

2. Do they sell any mushrooms?

Mark sells some mushrooms.

Lisa doesn't sell any mushrooms.

3. Do they get any cucumbers?

Ann gets some cucumbers.

Paul doesn't get any cucumbers.

4. Do they want some strawberries?

The girls want some strawberries.

The boys don't want any strawberries.

5. Do they have any lemons?

Seth has some lemons.

Alex doesn't have any lemons.

Exercise G

There are no vegetables in Mary's refrigerator. There are some old grapes and some green apples. Mary wants some carrots and broccoli. She doesn't want any mushrooms.

There is a store down the street. It's Mary's favorite store. It sells juicy fruit and beautiful vegetables. Mary goes to that store two times a week. The vegetables aren't expensive.

Mary loves the different peppers at the store. The store has green and red peppers. There aren't any yellow ones. She finds some green grapes. There are no purple grapes. Mary buys grapes, carrots and broccoli.

1. a. vegetables
2. b. grapes
3. c. carrots & broccoli
4. a. mushrooms
5. b. two times
6. b. not expensive
7. c. yellow
8. a. grapes

Lesson 17

Exercise A

1. non-count
2. non-count
3. count
4. count
5. non-count
6. count
7. non-count
8. count
9. non-count
10. non-count
11. count
12. non-count
13. non-count
14. non-count
15. count
16. non-count
17. count
18. count
19. count
20. non-count

Lesson 17

Exercise B

1. much	6. many
2. many	7. much
3. much	8. many
4. much	9. many
5. many	10. much

Exercise C

1. a little	6. a little
2. a few	7. a few
3. a few	8. a little
4. a little	9. a few
5. a little	10. a little

Exercise D

1. How much cheese is there?
2. How much cheese do you eat?
3. How much cheese are you eating?
4. How many potatoes are there?
5. How many potatoes do you wash?
6. How many potatoes are you washing?
7. How much pasta does he have?
8. How much milk is there?
9. How many eggs do you want?
10. How much bread do you want?

Exercise E

1. much, a lot of, much
2. much, much, a little
3. plenty, much, much
4. a few, many, a few

Exercise F

1. Is there any rice?

   There is plenty of rice.

   How much rice does Tom want?

   He wants a little rice.

2. Are there any eggs?

   There are a lot of eggs.

   How many eggs do you eat?

   I eat a few eggs.

3. Is there any coffee?

   There is a little coffee.

   How much coffee do the teachers drink?

   They drink a lot of coffee.

4. Are there any apples?

   There are a lot of apples.

   How many apples do the girls get?

   They get a few apples.

5. Is there any pasta?

   There is plenty of pasta.

   How much pasta does grandmother prepare?

   She prepares enough pasta.

Exercise G

1. They have four children.
2. They eat in the dining room at night.
3. His favorite vegetable are carrots.
4. He drinks four cups of coffee a day.
5. He takes his coffee with a spoon of sugar and a little milk.
6. She is buying pineapples today.
7. She needs a few onions and some tomatoes for tonight.

Exercise H

Jane has guests at her new apartment. The guests are her parents. Jane is preparing meat and potatoes for dinner. Jane's mother is eating bread with a little cheese before dinner. Jane and her mother are drinking a little wine and talking. Jane's father is in the living room. He is watching television. Jane's father isn't drinking wine. He drinks a lot of tea.

Jane has plenty of good food for dinner. She has enough meat and potatoes for tonight. She is putting a big bowl of watermelon on the table. After dinner there is cake and ice cream for dessert. Jane doesn't have any coffee.

1. c. parents
2. b. meat
3. c. a little
4. a. living room
5. c. wine
6. a. plenty
7. b. watermelon
8. c. any

Lesson 18

Exercise A

1. pours
2. slices
3. mixes
4. blends
5. washes
6. fries
7. teaches
8. grinds
9. heats
10. grills
11. freezes
12. finishes
13. tries
14. chooses
15. studies
16. has
17. asks
18. uses
19. goes
20. does

Exercise B

1. heats
2. bakes
3. blends
4. stirs
5. grills
6. peels
7. boils
8. mixes
9. fries
10. sprinkles

Exercise C

1. Tom wants eggs because he is hungry.
2. Tom puts two eggs and a little milk into a bowl.
3. Tom mixes the eggs with a large spoon.
4. Tom pours the eggs into the pan after the butter melts.
5. Tom fries the eggs for two minutes.
6. Tom sprinkles his eggs with salt because eggs are tasty with salt.
7. Tom peels an orange.
8. Tom eats his food at the dining room table.

Exercise D

1. What is Tom grilling?
   He is grilling fish.
   Why is Tom grilling fish?
   He is grilling fish because he is hungry.
2. What are you frying?
   I am frying eggs.
   Why are you frying eggs?
   I am frying eggs because there is no meat.
3. What is Sally toasting?
   She is toasting bread.
   Why is Sally toasting bread?
   She is toasting bread because she likes toast.
4. What is Aunt Mary baking?
   She is baking a cake.
   Why is Aunt Mary baking a cake?
   She is baking a cake because it's Ann's birthday

Lesson 18

5. What is Carl heating?

He is heating the sauce.

Why is Carl heating the sauce?

He is heating the sauce because the pasta is ready.

Exercise E

1. Tom washes the pots.

He is washing the pots.

Wash the pots.

2. Ann mixes the fruit.

She is mixing the fruit.

Mix the fruit.

3. I pour the milk.

I am pouring the milk.

Pour the milk.

4. Ron studies in the library.

He is studying in the library.

Study in the library.

5. The oven bakes the bread.

It is baking the bread.

Bake the bread.

6. Karen fries the eggs.

She is frying the eggs

Fry the eggs.

7. You and Sonny boil the water.

You are boiling the water.

Boil the water.

8. Jill and I chop the onions.

We are chopping the onions.

Chop the onions.

9. The chefs grill the meat.

They are grilling the meat.

Grill the meat.

10. Grandmother freezes the fish.

She is freezing the fish.

Freeze the fish.

Exercise F

My **sister cooks** my favorite food on Saturdays. **She makes** spicy fish with white rice.

She cuts large pieces of fish. **She sprinkles** salt and pepper on the fish. After **she prepares** the fish, **my sister puts** the rice in boiling water. **She cooks** the rice in **her** big pot. **She melts** butter on a hot pan. **My sister fries** the fish with peppers and onions.

Before we eat, **my sister mixes** the rice, fish, peppers and onions in a bowl.

Exercise G

My name is Jane. My family bakes a cake every week. We try different cakes. My mother's favorite cake is apple cake. She uses red apples for her apple cake. I make the apple cake with green apples. My mother likes the red ones.

My sister makes small birthday cakes for her friends and family. She sprinkles a lot of coconut on her delicious birthday cakes . My sister takes her cakes to school every week. Her teachers love her cakes.

My favorite cake is carrot cake. I use brown sugar and white sugar in my carrot cake. The cake takes four eggs and three carrots. I chop the carrots with a knife. I use a little salt in my cake.

1. a. bakes

2. a. apple

3. b. red

4. a coconut

5. c. school

6. a. carrot

7. b. four

8. b. chopping

Lesson 19

Exercise A

1. was	**11.** were
2. Were	**12.** was
3. were	**13.** were
4. Was	**14.** was
5. were	**15.** Were
6. was	**16.** was
7. was	**17.** were
8. Was	**18.** was
9. were	**19.** were
10. was	**20.** Was

Exercise B

1. He was at the restaurant.

2. I was in the cafeteria.

3. They were expensive.

4. We were at the store

5. They were inside the oven.

6. You were in the back of the kitchen.

7. It was in the dessert aisle.

8. They were at the meat counter.

9. It was behind the coffee.

10. You were at the table.

Exercise C

1. The restaurant is closed today.

It was closed yesterday.

2. Mary isn't hungry today.

She wasn't hungry yesterday.

3. The rice isn't sweet today.

It wasn't sweet yesterday.

4. John's beans aren't spicy today.

They weren't spicy yesterday.

5. Katy and I are thirsty today.

We were thirsty yesterday.

6. The shrimp isn't grilled today.

It wasn't grilled yesterday.

7. The lemons aren't juicy today.

They weren't juicy yesterday.

8. The coffee is delicious today.

It was delicious yesterday.

9. The grill isn't on today.

It wasn't on yesterday.

10. The fries aren't salty today.

They weren't salty yesterday.

Exercise D

1. Were the eggs fried?

2. Was the chicken ready?

3. Were the grapes ripe?

4. Were the hamburgers delicious?

5. Was it next to the salt and pepper?

6. Was the bread on top of the shelf?

7. Was there a knife on the counter?

8. Was our grill behind the garage?

9. Was this butter expensive?

10. Were there pans in the sink?

Lesson 19

Exercise E

1. The strawberries were good.
   They weren't bad.
2. The cherries were sweet.
   They weren't sour.
3. The fries were baked.
   They weren't fried.
4. The steak wasn't greasy.
   It was juicy.
5. The bananas were delicious.
   They weren't terrible.
6. The grapes weren't sour.
   They weren't ripe.
7. The cucumber was long.
   It wasn't short.
8. The salad was large.
   It wasn't small.

Exercise F

1. What was for breakfast?
   Cereal was for breakfast.
   Were there any eggs?
   No, there weren't any eggs.
2. What was for lunch?
   Hamburgers were for lunch.
   Were there any fries?
   No, there weren't any fries.
3. What was for dinner?
   Steak was for dinner.
   Was there any shrimp?
   No, there wasn't any shrimp.
4. What was for dessert?
   Pie was for dessert.
   Was there any ice cream?
   No, there wasn't any ice cream.

5. What was for lunch?
   Sandwiches were for lunch.
   Was there any soup?
   No, there wasn't any soup.

Exercise G

Boy: Mom, I want a piece of chocolate cake for breakfast.

Mother: No, you aren't having chocolate cake for breakfast. There is cereal and milk. We have some fruit. I am making pancakes. Which of those do you prefer?

Boy: Mom, there are eggs in chocolate cake.

Mother: Son, you are not having chocolate cake. Please don't ask again.

Boy: Okay Mom. Were there two apples on the table yesterday?

Mother: Yes, there were. I put the apples in the refrigerator. Do you want an apple?

Boy: Yes, I want an apple and some pancakes with butter. Is there any toast?

Mother: We don't have slices of bread. There wasn't any bread at the store yesterday. Do you want me to slice your apple?

Boy: Yes, please. Mom, what are we having for dinner?

Mother: Your father was hungry for pasta. We are having shrimp and pasta.

Boy: I like shrimp in my pasta.

Mother: I know you do.

Boy: What are we having for dessert?

Mother: Do you want chocolate cake?

Boy: No, I want a cherry pie.

1. a. cake
2. b. pancakes
3. a. two
4. a. toast
5. b. wasn't
6. b. broccoli
7. c. shrimp
8. a. cherry

Lesson 20

Exercise A

1. loved
2. asked
3. showed
4. wanted
5. used
6. multiplied
7. looked
8. answered
9. picked
10. grabbed
11. finished
12. crossed
13. fried
14. stirred
15. shared
16. chopped
17. ended
18. lived
19. tried
20. worked

Exercise B

1. The server needed a tip.
2. We carried the trays to the kitchen.
3. Sheila enjoyed the chef's pasta.
4. You needed an appetizer.
5. I liked the bartender.
6. We removed the tips from the table.
7. They placed the plates on the trays.
8. The cashier closed the diner.
9. You stirred the drinks.
10. Andy and Kristen tasted the food.

Exercise C

1. Mary folds the napkins.
   She folded the napkins this morning.
2. The restaurant is closed.
   It was closed two weeks ago.
3. I serve the appetizers.
   I served the appetizers last night.
4. The bartender prepares the drinks
   He (She) she prepared the drinks for the customers.
5. Katy and I chop the onions.
   We chopped the onions first.
6. The chefs uses ripe vegetables.
   They used ripe vegetables last week.

Exercise D

1. The chef **grilled** the steaks on the kitchen grill.
2. My parents **enjoyed** a tasty lunch at the new diner.
3. I **carried** the tray back to the kitchen.
4. She **grabbed** the bill from the table.
5. The customers **ordered** from the menu.
6. The downtown cafe **closed** last year.
7. The appetizers **tasted** terrible.
8. The mother **sliced** the cake with a knife.
9. The server **answered** questions about the menu.
10. Alan **sprinkled** a lot of salt on his eggs.

Lesson 20

Exercise E

I **worked** at the diner on Tuesday night. Tuesday **was** a good night at the diner. The chef **served** appetizers to the cashiers and the servers. We **enjoyed** shrimp, fish and many tasty fruits.

For work I **removed** the dirty plates from the tables. I **placed** the clean forks and napkins for new customers. I **cleaned** the trays for the servers. I **washed** the cups and glasses for the bartender.

I **helped** the chef at 11:00 p.m. because the Cherry Diner **closed** at midnight. The chefs **cleaned** the grill, oven, counters and the kitchen floor. The bartenders **returned** the menus to the bar. I **stayed** after 12:00 p.m. on Tuesday night.

Exercise F

1. Where were you this morning?

   I was were at the cafe.

   I ordered a coffee.

2. Where was Tom at lunch.

   He was at the buffet.

   He tried a steak.

3. Where were the friends on Friday?

   They were at the bar.

   They enjoyed an appetizer.

4. Where was I on Monday.

   You were at the diner.

   You cleaned the grill.

5. Where were the servers yesterday.

   They were with the chef.

   They created the menu.

Exercise G

My name is Tony. Yesterday my family tried the new cafe across the street from the post office. We were excited. The cafe opened last month. We walked into the cafe and waited a few seconds for a seat. The cafe was clean. The customers looked happy.

The server showed my family to a big booth in the back of the dining room. We looked at the menu for a few minutes. The server was nice. He poured coffee for my mother and father. My parents stirred their coffee and added some milk. The chef stopped by and offered some bread.

I ordered eggs and bacon. My sister ordered pancakes with strawberries. My mother and father ordered omelets. The bacon and eggs were delicious. I helped my sister finish her pancakes. My family enjoyed the new cafe.

1. a. post office
2. b. month
3. a. clean
4. a. booth
5. c. poured
6. c. chef
7. a. eggs
8. a. enjoyed

Lesson 21

Exercise A

1. The wanted / They did not want / Did they want
2. I pushed / They did not push / Did they push
3. You went / They did not go / Did they go
4. We pulled / They did not pull / Did they pull
5. He opened / They did not open / Did they open
6. She had / They did not have / Did they have
7. You asked / They did not ask / Did they ask
8. They needed / They did not need / Did they need
9. We carried / They did not carry / Did they carry
10. I shopped / They did not shop / Did they shop

Exercise B

1. Did Mary want the mustard?

2. Did Alan shop with a cart?

3. Did they taste the yogurt?

4. Did you prepare the salad dressing?

5. Did you (we) share the nuts?

6. Did they move the soda?

7. Did Alice spill the vinegar?

8. Did Henry clean the jars?

9. Did I (we) use the right glass?

10. Did you finish the candy?

Exercise C

1. Did John go to the store today?
   No, he didn't go the store today.
   He went to the store yesterday.

2. Did Ana use the coupon yesterday?
   No, she didn't use the coupon yesterday.
   She used the coupon this morning.

3. Did Mark have the candy last week?
   No, he didn't have the candy last week.
   He had the candy yesterday.

4. Did you open the box today?
   No, I didn't open the box today.
   I opened the box 5 minutes ago.

5. Did they bake the cookies on Saturday.
   No, they didn't bake the cookies on Saturday.
   They baked the cookies yesterday.

6. Did Seth wash the bottles last Monday?
   No, he didn't wash the bottle last Monday.
   He washed the bottles this afternoon.

7. Did I do it before noon?
   No, you didn't do it before noon.
   You did it after 3 p.m.

Exercise D

1. They shopped for groceries **on Sunday.**

2. They went to **Savers Grocery Store**.

3. **Yes,** he **pushed** the cart through the store.

4. He grabbed **a box of cookies** on aisle six.

5. **No, there wasn't** an open register.

6. They waited in line **for 10 minutes**.

7. They paid **the cashier** for their food.

Exercise E

1. Did you open the yogurt?
   No, I didn't open the yogurt.
   What did you open?
   I opened the nuts.

2. Did Robert grill the hamburger?
   No, he didn't grill the hamburger.
   What did he grill?
   He grilled the steak.

3. Did Sheila taste the chicken?
   No, she didn't taste the chicken.
   What did she taste?
   She tasted the shrimp.

4. Did Tim and Pam enjoy the pie?
   No, they didn't enjoy the pie.
   What did Tim and Pam enjoy?
   They enjoyed the ice cream.

5. Did I order the sandwich?
   No, you didn't order the sandwich.
   What did I order?
   You ordered the soup.

Lesson 21

Exercise F

1. What did Tom have?
2. Where did Ann go?
3. Who did the cooking?
4. Where was Karen yesterday?
5. Who were you with?
6. Did they have a coupon?
7. Who did David go with?
8. Did you do it?
9. When were you there?
10. Did you have a cookie?

Exercise G

Emily and her sister Ally went to a diner for lunch yesterday. There were a lot of people in the restaurant. The server walked Emily and Ally to a booth near the window. They ordered two sodas.

Ally looked at the menu for a second. Emily was hungry. She ordered a hamburger with chips and a salad. She asked for the salad dressing in a small container. Ally wasn't hungry. She ordered a cup of soup.

Emily and Ally talked and waited for their food. They got their food after ten minutes. Emily squirted a little mustard on her hamburger. Ally sprinkled some salt in her soup.

1. b. lunch
2. c. a lot of
3. c. a window
4. c. soda
5. a. chips
6. a. container
7. c. soup
8. b. mustard

Lesson 22

Exercise A

1. high
2. short
3. far
4. shallow
5. short
6. wide
7. thin
8. soft
9. tiny
10. old

Exercise B

1. went
2. had
3. ate
4. burned
5. fixed
6. drank
7. tasted
8. came
9. needed
10. made

Exercise C

1. helped help/**t**/
2. switched switch/**t**/
3. burned burn/**d**/
4. shared share/**d**/
5. needed need/**id**/
6. moved move/**d**/
7. placed place/**t**/
8. tasted taste/**id**/
9. mixed mix/**t**/
10. measured measure/**d**/
11. added add/**id**/
12. stopped stop/**t**/
13. fixed fix/**t**/
14. peeled peel/**d**/
15. pushed push/**t**/
16. grabbed grab/**d**/
17. hugged hug/**d**/
18. suggested suggest/**id**/
19. cooked cook/**t**/
20. compared compare/**d**/

Exercise D

1. How long is the table?
   What is the length of the table?
2. How wide is the desk?
   What is the width of the desk?
3. How tall is Henry?
   What is the height of Henry?
4. How deep is the river?
   What is the depth of the river?
5. How high is the flag?
   What is the height of the flag?
6. How thick is the book?
   What is the thickness of the book?
7. How far away is the church?
   What is the distance to the church?

Exercise E

1. I **put** the fruit **on** the table.
2. He **made** eggs **for** lunch.
3. He **ate with** me yesterday.
4. I **cut** the straw **in** half.
5. She **drove the** long way.
6. She **brought a** thick book.
7. We **drank** a lot **of** tea.
8. It **came** close **to** me.

Exercise F

Steve **loved** his <u>old</u> house at the lake. The lake **was** <u>close to</u> his house. The **distance** from the house to the lake **was** about 500 feet.

Steve's uncle **measured** the **depth** of the lake every summer. The lake **was** very <u>deep</u> in July.

Steve **made** tables and chairs for his lake house. Two of the tables **were** 10 feet <u>long</u>. Steve **set** the **length** of the tables to 10 feet because he **had** a <u>big</u> family. The table tops **were** very <u>thick</u>. The **thickness was** about two inches.

Steve and his uncle **ate** lunch every day on the outside patio. They **took** their sandwiches and snacks to the <u>west</u> patio. Steve's uncle **cut** the sandwiches in quarters.

Exercise G

1. I measured the door.
   How wide is the door?
   The width is forty-eight inches.
   It isn't narrow.
2. I visited the bridge.
   How long is the bridge?
   The length is two kilometers.
   It isn't short.
3. I stopped at the lake.
   How deep is the lake?
   The depth is twenty-six feet.
   It isn't shallow.
4. I brought a book.
   How thick is the book?
   The thickness is four inches.
   It isn't thin.
5. I went to the church.
   How far is the church?
   The distance is twenty miles.
   It isn't close.

Lesson 22

Exercise H

1. needed   a. /id/
2. mixed   c. /t/
3. peeled   b. /d/
4. moved   b. /d/
5. placed   c. /t/
6. waited   a. /id/
7. cooked   c. /t/
8. tasted   a. /id/
9. grabbed   b. /d
10. shared   b. /d/

Exercise I

My name is Jacob. I have two shelves in my bedroom closet. There is a low shelf for my pants. The high shelf is for shirts and jackets. The distance from the floor to the low shelf is three feet. The distance from the floor to the high shelf is six and a half feet. The shelves are five feet long. The depth of the shelves are eighteen inches. They are about an inch thick. I measured the shelves because I am buying new ones today.

I drove to the home store near my house. It was a short trip. The store is about two miles away. I told the salesperson the size of my shelves. He went to the back of the store. He returned with three different kinds of shelves. I compared the shelves for a few minutes. I put the expensive ones in my cart.

1. b. closet
2. b. floor
3. a. long
4. c. thickness
5. a. shelves
6. a. drove
7. c. miles
8. b. expensive

Lesson 23

Exercise A

1. height
2. width
3. height
4. depth
5. direction
6. distance
7. distance
8. weight
9. depth
10. length
11. distance
12. weight
13. volume
14. size
15. weight
16. height
17. weight
18. length
19. size
20. height, length

Exercise B

1. He was running
   He was not running
   Was he running
2. They were filling
   They were not filling
   Were they filling
3. She was emptying
   She was not emptying
   Was she emptying
4. We were dropping
   We were not dropping
   Were we dropping
5. It was changing
   It was not changing
   Was it changing
6. You were pushing
   You were not pushing
   Were you pushing
7. They were pulling
   They were not pulling
   Were they pulling
8. I was being
   I was not being
   Was I being
9. He was scrubbing
   He was not scrubbing
   Was he scrubbing
10. We were trying
    We were not trying
    Were we trying

Exercise C

1. Sally didn't wipe the mirror with water.
   Sally was wiping the mirror with a cleaner.
2. Greg put the vacuum away.
   Greg wasn't putting the vacuum in the closet.
3. Gina scrubbed the sink with a sponge.
   Gina wasn't scrubbing the toilet with her hand.
4. The girls used a duster on the blinds.
   The boys were using a mop on the floor.
5. You took the dustpan to the garage.
   You weren't taking the bucket outside.
6. I swept the garage with the broom.
   I was sweeping the floor at noon.

Exercise D

1. Was he filling the buckets?
2. Was she moving the carts?
3. Were they getting the 2 liter bottle?
4. Was it working?
5. Were you using heavy weights?
6. Were they emptying the gallon buckets?
7. Was Tom visiting his mother?
8. Were you teaching math?
9. Were Bill and Sharon running fast?
10. Were you looking for the can?

Exercise E

1. What were you moving?
   I was moving a 5-gallon bottle.
   How much did the bottle weigh?
   It weighed 42 pounds.
2. What was John filling?
   He was filling a bucket.
   How much did the bucket weigh?
   It weighed 10 pounds.
3. What were the boys weighing?
   They were weighing a box.
   How much did the box weigh?
   It weighed 9 kilograms.
4. What were you buying?
   I was buying a table.
   How much did the table weigh?
   It weighed 140 pounds.
5. What was Mom getting?
   She was getting a cucumber.
   How much did the cucumber weigh?
   It weighed one ounce.

Exercise F

1. when
2. while
3. when
4. when
5. while
6. while
7. when
8. while
9. while
10. when

Exercise G

1. dropped
2. was preparing
3. spilled
4. were baking
5. told
6. came
7. was watching
8. was paying
9. was doing
10. asked

Lesson 23

Exercise H

Henry helped his aunt make tomato sauce yesterday. She was cleaning her quart containers for the sauce when Henry came to her house around noon. Henry grabbed one of the tomato buckets from the back patio. The bucket was very heavy. It weighed about twenty pounds.

Henry emptied the bucket of tomatoes in the sink. Henry's aunt cut onions for the sauce while he was washing the tomatoes with hot water.

Henry's aunt added nine tomatoes to her kitchen scale. The scale showed four pounds. At 12:30 they cut the tomatoes. It was time to cook the sauce.

1. a. aunt
2. c. quart
3. a. buckets
4. b. 20 lb.
5. c. emptied
6. a. cut
7. b. pounds
8. b. 12:30

Lesson 24

Exercise A

1. him, his
2. her, hers
3. me, mine
4. you, yours
5. us, ours
6. them, theirs
7. us, ours
8. them, theirs
9. them, theirs
10. them, theirs
11. them, theirs
12. her, hers
13. him, his
14. you, yours
15. it, its
16. it, its

Exercise B

1. it
2. him
3. me
4. her
5. us
6. them
7. it
8. you
9. it, him
10. her
11. him
12. them

Exercise C

1. I love this wrench.
This wrench is **mine**.
Bob gave the wrench to **me**.
2. **We** build with these tools.
These tool are **ours**.
Dad gave the tools to **us**.
3. This **electric saw** is dirty.
There is oil on **its** plug.
I need to wash **it**.
4. **John and Steve** have a red ladder.
This blue ladder is not **theirs**.
Ann gave **them** the red ladder.
5. **Melissa** needs a razor blade.
Is this razor blade **hers**?
Yes, I saw **her** with it.
6. **You** have pliers.
These pliers are **yours**.
Bob gave them to **you**.
7. **Robert** has nuts, bolts, and screws.
The nails are **his** too.
I asked **him** for two screws.
8. **Dave and I** have ten feet of rope.
The rope is **ours**.
Bob gave it to **us**.

Exercise D

1. Yes, **it** was **hers**.
Yes, **she** gave **it** to **him**.
2. Yes, **it** was **his**.
Yes, **he** gave **it** to **her**.
3. Yes, **they** were **his**.
Yes, **he** gave **them** to **him**.
4. Yes, **they** were **theirs**.
Yes, **they** gave **them** to **him**.
5. Yes, **it** was **hers**.
Yes, **she** gave **it** to **her**.

Exercise E

John **bought** a new power drill yesterday morning. He **got it** at a store downtown. John **talked** with his friend Dan while he **was shopping**. John **told him** about different types of tools.

This morning John **hung** new kitchen cabinet doors for his wife Mary. Mary **left** the kitchen while John **was tearing them** out. In the afternoon he **fixed** a bathroom outlet for **her**.

John's daughters **bent** a piece of metal on their dresser. In the evening John **worked** on **it** for **them**. He **built** a new drawer for the dresser.

Exercise F

1. Did Bob find a hammer for Lisa?

   Yes, he found a hammer for her.

   Whose hammer is it?

   It's his.

2. Did you get a ladder for Phil?

   Yes, I got a ladder for him.

   Whose ladder is it?

   It's mine.

3. Did you and I leave tools for the boys?

   Yes, we left tools for them.

   Whose tools are they?

   They're ours.

4. Did I bring wood for you?

   Yes, you brought wood for me.

   Whose wood is it?

   It's yours.

5. Did Sam and Kelly have nuts for the metal?

   Yes, they had nuts for it.

   Whose nuts are they?

   They're theirs.

Exercise G

My name is Chris. My brother Dan and I keep our tools in the garage. We build different things with our tools. We build tables, chairs and beds. We also build big wood clocks.

This power drill over here is Dan's. The electric saw on the counter is also his. The wrenches and pliers on these shelves are mine. My father gave me this hammer for my birthday. Danny bought me this wrench last week.

We keep our nuts, bolts, nails, and screws in little jars. We keep the wood on the shelves in the back.

1. c. brother
2. b. tools
3. a. clocks
4. b. saw
5. c. pliers
6. a. brought
7. c. nails
8. c. wood

Lesson 25

Exercise A

1. softer
2. nicer
3. bigger
4. easier
5. more beautiful
6. heavier
7. worse
8. sadder
9. closer
10. cuter
11. easier
12. happier
13. better
14. farther
15. more popular
16. prettier
17. fatter
18. shorter
19. dirtier
20. thinner

Lesson 25

Exercise B

1. The rooster is faster than the chicken.
2. The cat is softer than the dog.
3. The pig is dirtier than the donkey.
4. Jane is more beautiful than Mary.
5. Henry is taller than Greg.
6. The kitten is cuter than the puppy.
7. The cow is bigger than the sheep.
8. The hospital is closer than the church.
9. Division is easier than addition.
10. Marty is nicer than Steve.

Exercise C

1. Henry's dog is heavier than Alice's dog.
2. Judy's horse is older than Amy's horse.
3. Harry's pig is taller than Jim's pig.
4. Mary's cat is younger than John's cat.
5. The horse's tail is longer than the donkey's tail.
6. Alan is shorter than Teddy.
7. I walk farther than you walk.
8. My dog is lazier than your dog.
9. The rooster's tail feathers are longer than the chicken's tail feathers.
10. The kittens are more popular with the children than the cats.

Exercise D

1. Alice went to the ABC pet store on Saturday morning.
2. Yes, the puppies were noisier than the birds.
3. No, the cat collars were not more expensive than the dog collars.
4. Alice and her brother went to their grandparent's farm on Sunday.
5. Alice rode Trigger while Eric was feeding the chickens.
6. No, Trigger was not dirtier than the other farm animals.

Exercise E

1. Roosters are loud.
   Is a rooster louder than a chicken?
   Yes, a rooster is louder than a chicken.
   Chickens are quieter than roosters.
2. Pigs are dirty.
   Is a pig dirtier than a donkey?
   Yes, a pig is dirtier than a donkey.
   Donkeys are cleaner than pigs.
3. Dogs are big.
   Is a dog bigger than a puppy?
   Yes, a dog is bigger than a puppy.
   Puppies are smaller than dogs.
4. Paws are soft.
   Is a paw softer than a hoof?
   Yes, a paw is softer than a hoof.
   Hooves are harder than paws.
5. Horses are fast.
   Is a horse faster than a cow?
   Yes, a horse is faster than a cow.
   Cows are slower than horses.

Exercise F

My name is Gloria. I lived outside of Omaha on a big farm. We had two horses, two cows, two pigs, four chickens and one rooster. Our black horse was bigger than our brown horse. The two cows were white. They gave us milk. The pigs were both pink. One of the pigs had a long black stripe on his back. He was smaller than the other pig.

The chickens were all brown. The rooster was bigger than the chickens. Our rooster wasn't mean. He was very loud. He sat on the fence in the morning. There were lots of birds around our farm. I found lots of different colored feathers while walking our dog around the farm.

1. c. on a farm
2. c. four
3. a. bigger
4. b. white
5. b. smaller
6. c. loud
7. a. birds
8. a. feather

Lesson 26

Exercise A

1. shortest
2. closest
3. thinnest
4. deadliest
5. most careful
6. worst
7. tallest
8. cutest
9. biggest
10. smallest
11. scariest
12. largest
13. fattest
14. angriest
15. best
16. most
17. wildest
18. dirtiest
19. most beautiful
20. farthest

Exercise B

1. Wolves are fast.

   Tigers are faster than wolves.

   Lions are the fastest.

2. Rats are scary.

   Snakes are scarier than rats.

   Crocodiles are the scariest.

3. Monkeys are strong.

   Gorillas are stronger than rats.

   Bears are the strongest.

4. Rats are quick.

   Dogs are quicker than pigs.

   Cats are the quickest.

5. Snake are beautiful.

   Deer are more beautiful than snakes.

   Owls are the most beautiful.

6. Turtles are cute.

   Puppies are cuter than turtles.

   Kittens are the cutest.

Exercise C

1. The white bear is the oldest.

   The black bear is the youngest.

2. The giraffe is the tallest.

   The horse is the shortest.

3. The tiger is the heaviest.

   The dog is the lightest.

4. The elephant's tail is the longest.

   The donkey's tail is the shortest.

5. The crocodile has the most teeth.

   The cat has the least teeth.

6. The elephant is the strongest.

   The dog is the weakest.

7. Bears are the fastest.

   Turtles are the slowest.

8. Rudy's house is the farthest.

   Erin's house is the closest.

9. I am the oldest.

   Ellen is the youngest.

10. The white shell is the best.

    The red shell is the worst.

Exercise D

1. How deadly are these animals?

   Snakes are deadly animals.

   Crocodiles are deadlier than snakes.

   Lions are the deadliest of all these animals.

2. How quick are these birds?

   Roosters are quick birds.

   Owls are quicker than roosters.

   Eagles are the quickest of all these birds.

3. How smart are these pets?

Horses are smart pets.

Cats are smarter than horses.

Dogs are the smartest of all these pets.

4. How dirty are these animals?

Rats are dirty animals.

Donkeys are dirtier than rats.

Pigs are the dirtiest of all these animals.

5. How expensive are these tools?

Ladders are expensive tools.

Power drills are more expensive than ladders.

Electric saws are the most expensive of all these tools.

Exercise E

1. It was the best trip of his life.

2. It was the most beautiful animal they saw on their first day.

3. She saw the owl sitting on a tree branch near the river.

4. They were the biggest ones in the park.

5. He told Andy the worst animals in the park were bears and snakes.

6. It was the scariest day of his life because they saw three bears less than 30 feet away.

Exercise F

My name is Andrea. I love my pets. I have a dog, a cat, and a small turtle. The dog is the biggest of my three pets. My cat is bigger than my turtle. The turtle is the smallest of my three pets. He is also the quietest. My dog's name is Wolf. When he was a puppy, he looked like a gray wolf.

I like studying about animals in the wild. I saw a wolf at the National Park last year. Wolves are big. They aren't as big as bears. I think bears are one of the scariest wild animals. At my school we study about giraffes, lions, and tigers. Tigers are one of the fastest animals. Giraffes are the tallest animals.

1. c. turtle	**5.** c. National Park
2. a. biggest	**6.** a. scary
3. c. a & b	**7.** a. tigers
4. b. wolf	**8.** b. tallest

Lesson 27

Exercise A

1. swam	**11.** came
2. made	**12.** hit
3. flew	**13.** built
4. gave	**14.** brought
5. understood	**15.** bent
6. drank	**16.** told
7. found	**17.** ate
8. kept	**18.** got
9. lost	**19.** tore
10. left	**20.** broke

Exercise B

1. Butterflies are not as small as mosquitoes.

2. Spiders are not as noisy as bees.

3. Sharks are not as gentle as dolphins.

4. Flies are not as beautiful as butterflies.

5. Octopuses are not as big as whales.

6. Grasshoppers are not as gross as fleas.

7. Penguins are not as fast as seals.

8. Snakes are not as silent as mosquitoes.

Exercise C

1. The whale is not as dangerous as the shark.

2. Sharks are not as friendly as dolphins.

3. The spider web is not as beautiful as the sea coral.

4. Molly's puppy is not as cute as Harry's puppy.

5. The donkey is not as fast as the horse.

6. Your dogs are not as gentle as my dogs.

7. The black pigs are not as dirty as the pink pigs.

8. The spider web is not as big as the bee hive.

9. Jellyfish are not as quick as octopuses.

10. The hammer is not as expensive as the electric drill.

Exercise D

1. No, dolphins are not as aggressive as sharks and whales.

2. No, sharks are not as large as whales.

3. Penguins and seals live in the ocean and on land.

4. Yes, seals are faster than penguins.

5. Octopus eat jellyfish and crabs.

6. Yes, turtles put their eggs in nests.

Exercise E

1. Are whales as mean as sharks?

   No, whales are not as mean as sharks.

   Sharks are a lot meaner than whales.

2. Are penguins as fast as seals?

   No, penguins are not as fast as seals.

   Seals are a little faster than penguins.

3. Are ants as noisy as crickets?

   No, ants are not as noisy as crickets.

   Crickets are much noisier than ants.

4. Are octopuses as deadly as snakes?

   No, octopuses are not as deadly as snakes.

   Snakes are a lot deadlier than octopuses.

5. Are crabs as scary as jellyfish?

   No, crabs are not as scary as jellyfish.

   Jellyfish are much scarier than crabs.

Exercise F

Barry studies insects at school. His favorite insects are bees and crickets. Bees are flying insects. Bees are not as scary as spiders. They are as dangerous as many common spiders.

Barry is careful when he sees a bee hive. He doesn't get close to the hive. Bees have four wings. Crickets have two wings. Crickets do not fly as good as bees. Barry catches crickets for fun.

He walks around the outside of his house looking for spider webs. The spider webs around Barry's house are bigger than the ones at his school. The spider webs around Barry's house are not as big as the bee hive in his yard. Barry's father removed the hive from the house. He was gentle with the bees.

1. c. school
2. a. crickets
3. a. as dangerous as
4. a. careful
5. b. spider webs
6. b. bigger
7. b. in
8. a. gentle

Lesson 28

Exercise A

1. slowly
2. carelessly
3. badly
4. carefully
5. differently
6. crazily
7. loosely
8. loudly
9. hard
10. honestly
11. beautifully
12. sadly
13 nicely
14. meanly
15. shyly
16. kindly
17. well
18. rudely
19. fast
20. lazily
21. weakly
22. tightly
23. terribly
24. simply
25. lightly
26. calmly
27. angrily
28. correctly
29. softly
30. heavily

Exercise B

1. adjective
2. adjective
3. adverb
4. adverb
5. adjective
6 adjective
7. adverb
8. adverb
9. adjective
10. adverb

Exercise C

1. good, well
2. bad, badly
3. simple, simply
4. loudly, loud
5. fast, fast
6. loosely, loose
7. kind, kindly
8. happy, happily
9. hard, hard
10. serious, seriously

Exercise D

1. The team ran on the field quickly.
2. The boy threw the ball fast.
3. The fans left the stadium slowly.
4. The team lost the game badly.
5. The referee spoke loudly to the coach.
6. The children played quietly.
7. John drove carefully to the game.
8. The girls put the balls away carelessly.
9. The principal quickly read the scores.
10. The coach kindly took us to the game.

Exercise E

1. He was the second best player on the team.
2. She made her players play hard.
3. They lost their last game because they weren't careful.
4. He lazily threw the ball to his teammate Chris.
5. They stood sadly on the court.
6. They politely left the court.

Exercise F

1. Is John aggressive on the field?
   No, he's not aggressive on the field.
   Jake is more aggressive than him.
   Jake plays aggressively on the field.
2. Is Alison fast on the court?
   No, she's not fast on the court.
   Andrea is faster than her.
   Andrea runs fast on the court.
3. Are the referees loud at the game?
   No, they're not loud at the game.
   The players are louder than them.
   The players talk loudly at the game.

4. Are you wild in the stadium?

No, I'm not wild in the stadium.

My uncle is wilder than me.

My uncle cheers wildly in the stadium.

5. Am I quiet in the classroom?

No, you're not quiet in the classroom.

Your brother is quieter than you.

Your brother reads quietly in the classroom.

Exercise G

Ruby loves sports. She plays three different sports at her school. Her team is the Eagles. Ruby is one of the best players on her soccer team. She always tries hard. She plays well most games.

Last night her school played against the Lions. Ruby easily scored two goals. The Lions lost badly. The score was five to zero.

Ruby's family watched the game calmly. They are big fans of the Eagles. Her family cheered crazily when Ruby scored her goals. They met Ruby on the field after the game. They hugged her tightly while telling her she played a great game.

1. b. three
2. c. Eagles
3. b. best
4. c. well
5. b. scored
6. a. calmly
7. a. crazily
8. c. tightly

Lesson 29

Exercise A

1. went
2. wore
3. ran
4. held
5. stood
6. won
7. tore
8. shot
9. caught
10. fit
11. blocked
12. sat
13. guarded
14. bought
15. dribbled
16. knew
17. surfed
18. wrote
19. skied
20. broke

Exercise B

1. John is surfing **today**.
2. My new cleats and bats arrive **soon**.
3. We are golfing **later**.
4. Yes, John plays tennis **tomorrow**.
5. Jerry is guarding the goal **now**.
6. We are surfing **tonight**.
7. They are coming **later**.
8. Eric surfs at the beach **early**.
9. I was playing volleyball **then**.
10. Lindsey skied down the hill **yesterday**.

Exercise C

1. John **always** surfs with his friends.
2. John **rarely** surfs in the morning.
3. I hit the ball hard **twice**.
4. Derrick **never** shoots the ball.
5. Ann **frequently** forgets her cleats.
6. I break a racket **weekly**.
7. Volleyball games begin **hourly**.
8. I **usually** ski at night.
9. Dan and Sharon golf **monthly**.
10. I yelled during the game **once**.

Lesson 29

Exercise D

1. The uniforms are **usually** clean.

   We **usually** wash them before the games.

2. The bats are **often** heavy.

   David **often** swings them before the games.

3. The helmets are **always** dirty.

   They **always** drop their helmets on the field.

4. The girls were at the park **daily**.

   They ran around the park **daily**.

5. Terry is **constantly** surfing.

   He surfed **constantly**.

6. The uniforms are **rarely** white.

   The players **rarely** wear white uniforms.

Exercise E

1. Sarah played golf one time this week.

   She **rarely** plays golf.

2. Billy shot the basketball three times this week.

   He **often** shoots the basketball.

3. Jackie stole the soccer ball seven times this week.

   She **always** steals the soccer ball.

4. The family lost the skis zero times this week.

   They **never** lose the skis.

5. Tim and I went to the stadium 6 times this week.

   We **frequently** go to the stadium.

Exercise F

1. When did John get his helmet?

   He got it yesterday.

   How often does he wear his helmet?

   He rarely wears it.

2. When did Ashley buy her clubs?

   She bought them recently.

   How often does she use her clubs?

   She frequently uses them.

3. When did Henry fix his surfboard?

   He fixed it today.

   How often does he clean his surfboard?

   He cleans it daily.

4. When did the players choose their uniforms?

   They chose them yesterday.

   How often do they wear their uniforms?

   They wear them weekly.

5. When did the girls use their rackets?

   They used them Tuesday.

   How often do they break their rackets?

   They never break them.

Exercise G

Tom plays three sports for his school. He plays soccer, basketball, and baseball. On his soccer team Tom usually guards the goal. He blocks the other team's shots. Tom always wears a red uniform for the soccer games.

Basketball is Tom's favorite sport. The players practice daily. The basketball games are twice a week. Tom dribbles the ball more than he shoots it. Tom's coach is never happy because Tom rarely shoots the ball.

In the Spring Tom plays baseball. The uniforms for the baseball team are usually white and blue. Tom owns two pairs of baseball cleats. The bats and helmets belong to the school. He's constantly swinging a bat. Tom hits the ball out of the park often.

1. a. baseball
2. c. uniform
3. a. daily
4. a. more than
5. c. never
6. a. blue
7. c. the school
8. b. often

Lesson 30

Exercise A

1. met	11. began
2. sold	12. rode
3. drove	13. forgot
4. shot	14. jumped
5. dove	15. beat
6. fit	16. tackled
7. fought	17. wore
8. fell	18. punched
9. led	19. held
10. bought	20. kicked

Exercise B

1. Did John win **something/anything**?
   No he didn't win **anything**.

2. Did Sheila drive **somewhere/anywhere**?
   Yes she drove **somewhere**.

3. Did Tony fight **someone/anyone/somebody/anybody**?
   No he didn't fight **anyone/anybody**.

4. Does John sell **something/anything**?
   Yes, he sells **something**.

5. Did the boys go **somewhere/anywhere**?
   Yes, they went **somewhere**.

6. Did the player tackle **someone/anyone/somebody/anybody**?
   No, he didn't tackle **anyone/anybody**.

7. Did Amanda throw **something/anything**?
   No, she didn't throw **anything**.

8. Is Alex skating **somewhere**?
   No, he isn't skating **anywhere**.

9. Did you forget **someone/anyone**?
   No, he didn't forget **anyone**.

10. Did you wear **something/anything**?
    Yes, I wore **something**.

Exercise C

1. He won **nothing**.

2. He said **nothing**.

3. **Nobody (No-one)** stretched.

4. They ran **everywhere** in the park.

5. Yes, the athletes ate **everything.**

6. I'm sorry, there is **nowhere** to skate here.

7. **Everybody (everyone)** raced today.

8. The tournaments are held **everywhere.**

9. **Nobody (No-one)** dove into the pool.

10. Yes, I brought **everything**.

Exercise D

1. No, I didn't find anything.

2. Yes, I saw someone.

3. No, I am not going anywhere.

4. Yes, I beat someone.

5. No, he didn't fight anyone.

6. Yes, I looked everywhere.

7. No, he didn't jump on anyone.

8. Yes, I forgot something.

9. No, I didn't race anywhere in the city.

10. Yes, I began something.

Exercise E

1. She went to a wrestling tournament at her brother's high school.

2. Her brother easily won four matches. He won a silver medal.

3. No, they do not let the athletes punch and kick.

4. She went to a skate park somewhere in Los Angeles.

5. She learned some new jumps at the skate park.

Lesson 30

Exercise F

1. Did everyone wrestle at the tournament?

Yes, everyone wrestled at the tournament.

Did anyone win a medal?

No, no-one won a medal.

2. Did anything help the offense?

Yes, something helped the offense.

Did anything help the defense?

No, nothing helped the defense.

3. Did anybody meet at the pool?

Yes, everybody met at the pool.

Did anybody practice at the track?"

No, nobody practiced at the track.

4. Did anyone beat the loser?

Yes, everyone beat the loser.

Did anyone punch the winner?

No, no-one punched the winner.

5. Did everybody cheer for the champion?

Yes, everybody cheered for the champion.

Did anybody stop the athlete?

No, nobody stopped the athlete.

Exercise G

My name is Jen. My soccer team practices daily on our home field. First everybody stretches for ten minutes. Next the whole team runs around the track four times.

At practice we work on our offense and defense. Everyone practices kicking goals. Someone always guards the goal. Today was my day. I dove for the ball many times. Nobody scored on me at first. Everyone was scoring goals on me near the end of practice.

There is a soccer tournament in San Diego next weekend. All of the teams are from California. Somebody told me that the winners get medals. I am looking forward to our first match. We usually play the tournament champions. They beat us last year.

1. b. daily   **5.** c. Someone

2. a. everybody   **6.** b. tournament

3. c. track   **7.** b. somebody

4. c. both   **8.** a. champions